THE SACRED WOOD

This was the first volume of Mr Eliot's criticism to be published, and it includes essays on Dante, Swinburne, Blake and the contemporaries of Shakespeare; on poetry, poetic drama and the criticism of poetry. They were the product of his early writing days and are especially interesting as evidence of Mr Eliot's ideas on literature at that time.

UNIVERSITY PAPERBACKS

U.P. II

The Sacred Wood

ESSAYS ON POETRY AND CRITICISM

BY

T. S. ELIOT

UNIVERSITY PAPERBACKS

METHUEN : LONDON
BARNES & NOBLE : NEW YORK

First published by Methuen & Co Ltd
4 November 1920, and reprinted eight times
First published in this series in 1960
Printed in Great Britain by
Butler & Tanner Ltd, Frome and London
Catalogue No. 2/6761/27

*University Paperbacks are published
by* METHUEN & CO LTD
*36 Essex Street, Strand, London WC2
and* BARNES & NOBLE INC
105 Fifth Avenue, New York 3

FOR H. W. E.

'Tacuit et fecit'

Certain of these essays appeared, in the same or a more primitive form, in *The Times Literary Supplement*, *The Athenæum*, *Art and Letters*, and *The Egoist*. The author desires to express his obligation to the editors of these periodicals.

PREFACE TO THE 1928 EDITION

I HAD intended, when the time came to prepare a second edition of this book, to revise some of the essays. I have found the task impossible, and perhaps even undesirable. For I discovered that what had happened in my own mind, in eight years, was not so much a change or reversal of opinions, as an expansion or development of interests. There are, it is true, faults of style which I regret ; and especially I detect frequently a stiffness and an assumption of pontifical solemnity which may be tiresome to many readers. But these, like the other faults of the book, are too well diffused throughout to be amended. I should have to write another book.

Indeed so much has happened, so many important books of critical theory and practice have appeared in these eight years, that the chief value remaining to this volume, if any, is as a document of its time : and that is another reason for altering nothing. The essays were written between the years 1917 and 1920 ; they represent therefore a transition between the period immediately before the war and the period since. Most of them were written during the brief and brilliant life of the *Athenæum* under

Mr. Middleton Murry; some of them directly at Mr. Murry's suggestion. Those were years in which we were struggling to revive old communications and to create new ones; and I believe that both Mr. Murry and myself are a little more certain of our directions than we were then.

It is an artificial simplification, and to be taken only with caution, when I say that the problem appearing in these essays, which gives them what coherence they have, is the problem of the integrity of poetry, with the repeated assertion that when we are considering poetry we must consider it primarily as poetry and not another thing. At that time I was much stimulated and much helped by the critical writings of Remy de Gourmont. I acknowledge that influence, and am grateful for it; and I by no means disown it by having passed on to another problem not touched upon in this book: that of the relation of poetry to the spiritual and social life of its time and of other times. This book is logically as well as chronologically the beginning; I do not, on the whole, repudiate it; so I beg the reader who has the benevolence to read it as something more than a mere collection of essays and reviews, to have the patience to consider it as an introduction to a larger and more difficult subject.

Poetry is a superior amusement: I do not mean an amusement for superior people. I call it an amusement, an amusement *pour distraire les honnêtes gens*, not because that is a true definition, but because if you call it anything else you are likely to call it something still more false.   If we think of the nature of amusement, then poetry is not amusing ; but if we think of anything else that poetry may seem to be, we are led into far greater difficulties.   Our definition of the use of one kind of poetry may not exhaust its uses, and will probably not apply to some other kind ; or if our definition applies to all poetry, it becomes so general as to be meaningless.   It will not do to talk of " emotion recollected in tranquillity," which is only one poet's account of his recollection of his own methods ;   or to call it a " criticism of life," than which no phrase can sound more frigid to anyone who has felt the full surprise and elevation of a new experience of poetry.   And certainly poetry is not the inculcation of morals, or the direction of politics ; and no more is it religion or an equivalent of religion, except by some monstrous abuse of words.   And certainly poetry is something over and above, and something quite different from, a collection of psychological data about the minds of poets, or about the history of an epoch ; for we could not take it even as that unless we had already assigned to it a value merely as poetry.

Hence, in criticizing poetry, we are right if we begin, with what sensibility and what knowledge of other poetry we possess, with poetry as excellent words in excellent arrangement and excellent metre.   That is what is called the technique of verse.   But we observe that we cannot define even the technique of verse ; we cannot say at what point " technique " begins or where it ends ; and if we

add to it a " technique of feeling," that glib phrase
will carry us but little farther. We can only say
that a poem, in some sense, has its own life ; that its
parts form something quite different from a body of
neatly ordered biographical data ; that the feeling,
or emotion, or vision, resulting from the poem is
something different from the feeling or emotion or
vision in the mind of the poet.

On the other hand, poetry as certainly has something to do with morals, and with religion, and even
with politics perhaps, though we cannot say what.
If I ask myself (to take a comparison on a higher
plane) why I prefer the poetry of Dante to that
of Shakespeare, I should have to say, because it
seems to me to illustrate a saner attitude towards
the mystery of life. And in these questions, and
others which we cannot avoid, we appear already
to be leaving the domain of criticism of " poetry."
So we cannot stop at any point. The best that we
can hope to do is to agree upon a point from
which to start, and that is, in part, the subject of
this book.

T. S. E.

March, 1928

INTRODUCTION

TO anyone who is at all capable of experiencing the pleasures of justice, it is gratifying to be able to make amends to a writer whom one has vaguely depreciated for some years. The faults and foibles of Matthew Arnold are no less evident to me now than twelve years ago, after my first admiration for him ; but I hope that now, on re-reading some of his prose with more care, I can better appreciate his position. And what makes Arnold seem all the more remarkable is, that if he were our exact contemporary, he would find all his labour to perform again. A moderate number of persons have engaged in what is called " critical " writing, but no conclusion is any more solidly established than it was in 1865. In the first essay in the first *Essays in Criticism* we read that

it has long seemed to me that the burst of creative activity in our literature, through the first quarter of this century, had about it in fact something premature ; and that from this cause its productions are doomed, most of them, in spite of the sanguine hopes which accompanied and do still accompany them, to prove hardly more lasting than the productions of far less splendid epochs. And this prematureness comes from its having proceeded without having its proper data, without sufficient material to work with. In other words, the English poetry of the first quarter of this century, with plenty of energy, plenty of creative force, did not know enough. This makes Byron so empty of matter, Shelley so incoherent, Wordsworth even, profound as he is, yet so wanting in completeness and variety.

This judgment of the Romantic Generation has not, so far as I know, ever been successfully controverted ; and it has not, so far as I know, ever made very much impression on popular opinion. Once a poet is accepted, his reputation is seldom disturbed, for better or worse. So little impression has Arnold's opinion made, that his statement will probably be as true of the first quarter of the twentieth century as it was of the nineteenth. A few sentences later, Arnold articulates the nature of the malady :

In the Greece of Pindar and Sophocles, in the England of Shakespeare, the poet lived in a current of ideas in the highest degree animating and nourishing to the creative power ; society was, in the fullest measure, permeated by fresh thought, intelligent and alive ; and this state of things is the true basis for the creative power's exercise, in this it finds its data, its materials, truly ready for its hand ; all the books and reading in the world are only valuable as they are helps to this.

At this point Arnold is indicating the centre of interest and activity of the critical intelligence ; and it is at this perception, we may almost say, that

Arnold's critical activity stopped. In a society in which the arts were seriously studied, in which the art of writing was respected, Arnold might have become a critic. How astonishing it would be, if a man like Arnold had concerned himself with the art of the novel, had compared Thackeray with Flaubert, had analysed the work of Dickens, had shown his contemporaries exactly why the author of *Amos Barton* is a more *serious* writer than Dickens, and why the author of *La Chartreuse de Parme* is more serious than either ? In *Culture and Anarchy*, in *Literature and Dogma*, Arnold was not occupied so much in establishing a criticism as in attacking the uncritical. The difference is that while in constructive work something can be done, destructive work must incessantly be repeated ; and furthermore Arnold, in his destruction, went for game outside of the literary preserve altogether, much of it political game untouched and inviolable by ideas. This activity of Arnold's we must regret ; it might perhaps have been carried on as effectively, if not quite so neatly, by some disciple (had there been one) in an editorial position on a newspaper. Arnold is not to be blamed : he wasted his strength, as men of superior ability sometimes do, because he saw something to be done and no one else to do it. The temptation, to any man who is interested in ideas and primarily in literature, to put literature into the corner until he cleaned up the whole country first, is almost irresistible. Some persons, like Mr. Wells and Mr. Chesterton, have succeeded so well in this latter profession of setting the house in order, and have attracted so much more attention than Arnold, that we must conclude that it is indeed their proper rôle, and that they have done well for themselves in laying literature aside.

Not only is the critic tempted outside of criticism. The criticism proper betrays such poverty of ideas and such atrophy of sensibility that men who ought to preserve their critical ability for the improvement of their own creative work are tempted into criticism. I do not intend from this the usually silly inference that the " Creative " gift is " higher " than the critical. When one creative mind is better than another, the reason often is that the better is the more critical. But the great bulk of the work of criticism could be done by minds of the second order, and it is just these minds of the second order that are difficult to find. They are necessary for the rapid circulation of ideas. The periodical press— the ideal literary periodical—is an instrument of transport ; and the literary periodical press is dependent upon the existence of a sufficient number of second-order (I do not say " second-rate," the word is too derogatory) minds to supply its material. These minds are necessary for that " current of ideas," that " society permeated by fresh thought," of which Arnold speaks.

It is a perpetual heresy of English culture to believe that only the first-order mind, the Genius, the Great Man, matters ; that he is solitary, and produced best in the least favourable environment, perhaps the Public School; and that it is most likely a sign of inferiority that Paris can show so many minds of the second order. If too much bad verse is published in London, it does not occur to us to raise our standards, to do anything to educate the poetasters; the remedy is, Kill them off. I quote from Mr. Edmund Gosse : [1]

Unless something is done to stem this flood of poetastry the art of verse will become not merely superfluous, but ridiculous. Poetry is not a formula which a thousand flappers and hobbledehoys ought to be able to master in a week without any training, and the mere fact that it seems to be now practised with such universal ease is enough to prove that something has gone amiss with our standards. . . . This is all wrong, and will lead us down into the abyss like so many Gadarene swine unless we resist it.

We quite agree that poetry is not a formula. But what does Mr. Gosse propose to do about it ? If Mr. Gosse had found himself in the flood of poetastry in the reign of Elizabeth, what would he have done about it ? would he have stemmed it ? What exactly is this abyss ? and if something " has gone amiss with our standards," is it wholly the fault of the younger generation that it is aware of no authority that it must respect ? It is part of the business of the critic to preserve tradition—where a good tradition exists. It is part of his business to see literature steadily and to see it whole ; and

[1] *Sunday Times,* May 30, 1920.

this is eminently to see it *not* as consecrated by
time, but to see it beyond time ; to see the best
work of our time and the best work of twenty-five
hundred years ago with the same eyes.[1]   It is part
of his business to help the poetaster to understand
his own limitations.   The poetaster who understands
his own limitations will be one of our useful second-
order minds ; a good minor poet (something which
is very rare) or another good critic.   As for the
first-order minds, when they happen, they will
be none the worse off for a " current of ideas " ;
the solitude with which they will always and everywhere be invested is a very different thing from
isolation, or a monarchy of death.

NOTE.—I may commend as a model to critics who
desire to correct some of the poetical vagaries of the
present age, the following passage from a writer who
cannot be accused of flaccid leniency, and the justice
of whose criticism must be acknowledged even by those
who feel a strong partiality toward the school of poets
criticized :—

" Yet great labour, directed by great abilities, is never
wholly lost ; if they frequently threw away their wit
upon false conceits, they likewise sometimes struck out
unexpected truth : if their conceits were far-fetched,
they were often worth the carriage.   To write on their
plan, it was at least necessary to read and think.   No
man could be born a metaphysical poet, nor assume the
dignity of a writer, by descriptions copied from descrip-

[1] Arnold, it must be admitted, gives us often the impression of seeing the masters, whom he quotes, as canonical
literature, rather than as masters.

tions, by imitations borrowed from imitations, by traditional imagery, and hereditary similes, by readiness of rhyme, and volubility of syllables.

" In perusing the works of this race of authors, the mind is exercised either by recollection or inquiry : something already learned is to be retrieved, or something new is to be examined. If their greatness seldom elevates, their acuteness often surprises ; if the imagination is not always gratified, at least the powers of reflection and comparison are employed ; and in the mass of materials which ingenious absurdity has thrown together, genuine wit and useful knowledge may be sometimes found buried perhaps in grossness of expression, but useful to those who know their value ; and such as, when they are expanded to perspicuity, and polished to elegance, may give lustre to works which have more propriety though less copiousness of sentiment."—JOHNSON, *Life of Cowley*.

" INTRAVIT pinacothecam senex canus, exercitati vultus et qui videretur nescio quid magnum promittere, sed cultu non proinde speciosus, ut facile appareret eum ex hac nota litteratum esse, quos odisse divites solent . . . ' ego ' inquit ' poeta sum et ut spero, non humillimi spiritus, si modo coronis aliquid credendum est, quas etiam ad immeritos deferre gratia solet.' "—PETRONIUS.

" I also like to dine on becaficas."

CONTENTS

xix

THE SACRED WOOD

THE PERFECT CRITIC

I

" Eriger en lois ses impressions personnelles, c'est le grand effort d'un homme s'il est sincère."—Lettres à 'Amazone.

COLERIDGE was perhaps the greatest of English critics, and in a sense the last. After Coleridge we have Matthew Arnold; but Arnold—I think it will be conceded—was rather a propagandist for criticism than a critic, a popularizer rather than a creator of ideas. So long as this island remains an island (and we are no nearer the Continent than were Arnold's contemporaries) the work of Arnold will be important; it is still a bridge across the Channel, and it will always have been good sense. Since Arnold's attempt to correct his countrymen, English criticism has followed two directions. When a distinguished critic observed recently, in a newspaper article, that " poetry is the most highly organized form of intellectual activity," we were conscious that we were reading neither Coleridge nor Arnold. Not only have the words " organized " and " activity,"

occurring together in this phrase, that familiar
vague suggestion of the scientific vocabulary which
is characteristic of modern writing, but one asked
questions which Coleridge and Arnold would not
have permitted one to ask. How is it, for instance, that poetry is more "highly organized"
than astronomy, physics, or pure mathematics,
which we imagine to be, in relation to the scientist
who practises them, "intellectual activity" of a
pretty highly organized type? "Mere strings of
words," our critic continues with felicity and truth,
"flung like dabs of paint across a blank canvas,
may awaken surprise . . . but have no significance whatever in the history of literature." The
phrases by which Arnold is best known may be
inadequate, they may assemble more doubts than
they dispel, but they usually have some meaning.
And if a phrase like "the most highly organized
form of intellectual activity" is the highest organiza-
tion of thought of which contemporary criticism,
in a distinguished representative, is capable, then,
we conclude, modern criticism is degenerate.

The verbal disease above noticed may be reserved
for diagnosis by and by. It is not a disease from
which Mr. Arthur Symons (for the quotation was,
of course, not from Mr. Symons) notably suffers.
Mr. Symons represents the other tendency; he
is a representative of what is always called "æsthetic
criticism" or "impressionistic criticism." And it
is this form of criticism which I propose to examine
at once. Mr. Symons, the critical successor of

Pater, and partly of Swinburne (I fancy that the phrase "sick or sorry" is the common property of all three), *is* the "impressionistic critic." He, if anyone, would be said to expose a sensitive and cultivated mind—cultivated, that is, by the accumulation of a considerable variety of impressions from all the arts and several languages—before an "object"; and his criticism, if anyone's, would be said to exhibit to us, like the plate, the faithful record of the impressions, more numerous or more refined than our own, upon a mind more sensitive than our own. A record, we observe, which is also an interpretation, a translation; for it must itself impose impressions upon us, and these impressions are as much created as transmitted by the criticism. I do not say at once that this is Mr. Symons; but it is the "impressionistic" critic, and the impressionistic critic is supposed to be Mr. Symons.

At hand is a volume which we may test.[1] Ten of these thirteen essays deal with single plays of Shakespeare, and it is therefore fair to take one of these ten as a specimen of the book:

Antony and Cleopatra is the most wonderful, I think, of all Shakespeare's plays . . .

and Mr. Symons reflects that Cleopatra is the most wonderful of all women:

The queen who ends the dynasty of the Ptolemies

---

[1] *Studies in Elizabethan Drama.* By Arthur Symons.

has been the star of poets, a malign star shedding baleful light, from Horace and Propertius down to Victor Hugo ; and it is not to poets only . . .

What, we ask, is this for ? as a page on Cleopatra, and on her possible origin in the dark lady of the Sonnets, unfolds itself. And we find, gradually, that this is not an essay on a work of art or a work of intellect ; but that Mr. Symons is living through the play as one might live it through in the theatre ; recounting, commenting :

In her last days Cleopatra touches a certain eleva- tion . . . she would die a thousand times, rather than live to be a mockery and a scorn in men's mouths . . . she is a woman to the last . . . so she dies . . . the plays ends with a touch of grave pity . . .

Presented in this rather unfair way, torn apart like the leaves of an artichoke, the impressions of Mr. Symons come to resemble a common type of popular literary lecture, in which the stories of plays or novels are retold, the motives of the characters set forth, and the work of art therefore made easier for the beginner. But this is not Mr. Symons' reason for writing. The reason why we find a similarity between his essay and this form of education is that *Antony and Cleopatra* is a play with which we are pretty well acquainted, and of which we have, therefore, our own impressions. We can please ourselves with our own impressions of the characters and their emotions ; and we do not find the impressions of another person, however sensitive, very significant. But if we can recall the time when we were ignorant of the French symbolists, and met with *The Symbolist Movement in Literature*, we remember that book as an introduction to wholly new feelings, as a revelation. After we have read Verlaine and Laforgue and Rimbaud and return to Mr. Symons' book, we may find that our own impressions dissent from his. The book has not, perhaps, a permanent value for the one reader, but it has led to results of permanent importance for him.

The question is not whether Mr. Symons' impressions are " true " or " false." So far as you can isolate the " impression," the pure feeling, it is, of course, neither true nor false. The point is that you never rest at the pure feeling ; you react in one of two ways, or, as I believe Mr. Symons does, in a mixture of the two ways. The moment you try to put the impressions into words, you either begin to analyse and construct, to " ériger en lois," or you begin to create something else. It is significant that Swinburne, by whose poetry Mr. Symons may at one time have been influenced, is one man in his poetry and a different man in his criticism ; to this extent and in this respect only, that he is satisfying a different impulse ; he is criticizing, expounding, arranging. You may say this is not the criticism of a critic, that it is emotional, not intellectual—though of this there are two opinions, but it is in the direction of analysis and construction, a beginning to " ériger en lois," and not

in the direction of creation. So I infer that Swinburne found an adequate outlet for the creative
impulse in his poetry ; and none of it was forced
back and out through his critical prose. The
style of the latter is essentially a prose style ; and
Mr. Symons' prose is much more like Swinburne's
poetry than it is like his prose. I imagine—
though here one's thought is moving in almost
complete darkness—that Mr. Symons is far more
disturbed, far more profoundly affected, by his
reading than was Swinburne, who responded rather
by a violent and immediate and comprehensive
burst of admiration which may have left him
internally unchanged. The disturbance in Mr.
Symons is almost, but not quite, to the point of
creating ; the reading sometimes fecundates his
emotions to produce something new which is not
criticism, but is not the expulsion, the ejection, the
birth of creativeness.

The type is not uncommon, although Mr. Symons
is far superior to most of the type. Some writers
are essentially of the type that reacts in excess of
the stimulus, making something new out of the
impressions, but suffer from a defect of vitality
or an obscure obstruction which prevents nature
from taking its course. Their sensibility alters the
object, but never transforms it. Their reaction is
that of the ordinary emotional person developed
to an exceptional degree. For this ordinary
emotional person, experiencing a work of art, has
a mixed critical and creative reaction. It is made

up of comment and opinion, and also new emotions which are vaguely applied to his own life. The sentimental person, in whom a work of art arouses all sorts of emotions which have nothing to do with that work of art whatever, but are accidents of personal association, is an incomplete artist. For in an artist these suggestions made by a work of art, which are purely personal, become fused with a multitude of other suggestions from multitudinous experience, and result in the production of a new object which is no longer purely personal, because it is a work of art itself.

It would be rash to speculate, and is perhaps impossible to determine, what is unfulfilled in Mr. Symons' charming verse that overflows into his critical prose. Certainly we may say that in Swinburne's verse the circuit of impression and expression is complete ; and Swinburne was therefore able, in his criticism, to be more a critic than Mr. Symons. This gives us an intimation why the artist is—each within his own limitations—oftenest to be depended upon as a critic ; his criticism will be criticism, and not the satisfaction of a suppressed creative wish—which, in most other persons, is apt to interfere fatally.

Before considering what the proper critical re-action of artistic sensibility is, how far criticism is " feeling " and how far " thought," and what sort of " thought " is permitted, it may be instructive to prod a little into that other temperament, so different from Mr. Symons', which issues in generalities such as that quoted near the beginning of this article.

II

" L'écrivain de style abstrait est presque toujours un sentimental, du moins un sensitif. L'écrivain artiste n'est presque jamais un sentimental, et très rarement un sensitif."
—*Le Problème du Style*.

The statement already quoted, that " poetry is the most highly organized form of intellectual activity," may be taken as a specimen of the abstract style in criticism. The confused distinction which exists in most heads between " abstract " and " concrete " is due not so much to a manifest fact of the existence of two types of mind, an abstract and a concrete, as to the existence of another type of mind, the verbal, or philosophic. I, of course, do not imply any general condemnation of philsophy ; I am, for the moment, using the word " philosophic " to cover the unscientific ingredients of philosophy ; to cover, in fact, the greater part of the philosophic output of the last hundred years. There are two ways in which a word may be " abstract." It may have (the word " activity," for example) a meaning which cannot be grasped by appeal to any of the senses ; its apprehension may require a deliberate suppression of analogies of visual or muscular experience, which is none the less an effort of imagination. " Activity " will mean for the trained scientist, if he employ the term, either nothing at all or something still more exact than anything it suggests to us. If we are allowed to accept certain remarks of Pascal and Mr. Bertrand Russell about mathematics, we believe that the mathematician deals with objects—if he will permit us to call them objects—which directly affect his sensibility. And during a good part of history the philosopher endeavoured to deal with objects which he believed to be of the same exactness as the mathematician's. Finally Hegel arrived, and if not perhaps the first, he was certainly the most prodigious exponent of emotional systematization, dealing with his emotions as if they were definite objects which had aroused those emotions. His followers have as a rule taken for granted that words have definite meanings, overlooking the tendency of words to become indefinite emotions. (No one who had not witnessed the event could imagine the conviction in the tone of Professor Eucken as he pounded the table and exclaimed *Was ist Geist? Geist ist . . .*) If verbalism were confined to professional philosophers, no harm would be done. But their corruption has extended very far. Compare a mediæval theologian or mystic, compare a seventeenth-century preacher, with any "liberal" sermon since Schleiermacher, and you will observe that words have changed their meanings. What they have lost is definite, and what they have gained is indefinite.

The vast accumulations of knowledge—or at least of information—deposited by the nineteenth century have been responsible for an equally vast ignorance.

When there is so much to be known, when there are so many fields of knowledge in which the same words are used with different meanings, when every one knows a little about a great many things, it becomes increasingly difficult for anyone to know whether he knows what he is talking about or not. And when we do not know, or when we do not know enough, we tend always to substitute emotions for thoughts. The sentence so frequently quoted in this essay will serve for an example of this process as well as any, and may be profitably contrasted with the opening phrases of the *Posterior Analytics*. Not only all knowledge, but all feeling, is in perception. The inventor of poetry as the most highly organized form of intellectual activity was not engaged in perceiving when he composed this definition ; he had nothing to be aware of except his own emotion about " poetry." He was, in fact, absorbed in a very different " activity " not only from that of Mr. Symons, but from that of Aristotle.

Aristotle is a person who has suffered from the adherence of persons who must be regarded less as his disciples than as his sectaries. One must be firmly distrustful of accepting Aristotle in a canonical spirit ; this is to lose the whole living force of him. He was primarily a man of not only remarkable but universal intelligence ; and universal intelligence means that he could apply his intelligence to anything. The ordinary intelligence is good only for certain classes of objects ; a brilliant man of science, if he is interested in poetry at all, may conceive grotesque judgments : like one poet because he reminds him of himself, or another because he expresses emotions which he admires ; he may use art, in fact, as the outlet for the egotism which is suppressed in his own speciality. But Aristotle had none of these impure desires to satisfy ; in whatever sphere of interest, he looked solely and steadfastly at the object ; in his short and broken treatise he provides an eternal example—not of laws, or even of method, for there is no method except to be very intelligent, but of intelligence itself swiftly operating the analysis of sensation to the point of principle and definition.

It is far less Aristotle than Horace who has been the model for criticism up to the nineteenth century. A precept, such as Horace, or Boileau gives us, is merely an unfinished analysis. It appears as a law, a rule, because it does not appear in its most general form ; it is empirical. When we understand necessity, as Spinoza knew, we are free because we assent. The dogmatic critic, who lays down a rule, who affirms a value, has left his labour incomplete. Such statements may often be justifiable as a saving of time ; but in matters of great importance the critic must not coerce, and he must not make judgments of worse and better. He must simply elucidate : the reader will form the correct judgment for himself.

And again, the purely " technical " critic—the critic, that is, who writes to expound some novelty

or impart some lesson to practitioners of an art
—can be called a critic only in a narrow sense.
He may be analysing perceptions and the means for
arousing perceptions, but his aim is limited and
is not the disinterested exercise of intelligence.
The narrowness of the aim makes easier the detec-
tion of the merit or feebleness of the work ; even
of these writers there are very few—so that their
" criticism " is of great importance within its
limits. So much suffices for Campion. Dryden is
far more disinterested ; he displays much free
intelligence ; and yet even Dryden—or any *literary*
critic of the seventeenth century—is not quite a
free mind, compared, for instance, with such a mind
as Rochefoucauld's. There is always a tendency to
legislate rather than to inquire, to revise accepted
laws, even to overturn, but to reconstruct out of
the same material. And the free intelligence is
that which is wholly devoted to inquiry.

Coleridge, again, whose natural abilities, and some
of whose performances, are probably more remarkable than those of any other modern critic, cannot
be estimated as an intelligence completely free.
The nature of the restraint in his case is quite
different from that which limited the seventeenth-
century critics, and is much more personal. Coleridge's metaphysical interest was quite genuine, and
was, like most metaphysical interest, an affair of
his emotions. But a literary critic should have no
emotions except those immediately provoked by a
work of art—and these (as I have already hinted)

are, when valid, perhaps not to be called emotions at all. Coleridge is apt to take leave of the data of criticism, and arouse the suspicion that he has been diverted into a metaphysical hare-and-hounds. His end does not always appear to be the return to the work of art with improved perception and intensified, because more conscious, enjoyment; his centre of interest changes, his feelings are impure. In the derogatory sense he is more "philosophic" than Aristotle. For everything that Aristotle says illuminates the literature which is the occasion for saying it; but Coleridge only now and then. It is one more instance of the pernicious effect of emotion.

Aristotle had what is called the scientific mind— a mind which, as it is rarely found among scientists except in fragments, might better be called the intelligent mind. For there is no other intelligence than this, and so far as artists and men of letters are intelligent (we may doubt whether the level of intelligence among men of letters is as high as among men of science) their intelligence is of this kind. Sainte-Beuve was a physiologist by training; but it is probable that his mind, like that of the ordinary scientific specialist, was limited in its interest, and that this was not, primarily, an interest in art. If he was a critic, there is no doubt that he was a very good one; but we may conclude that he earned some other name. Of all modern critics, perhaps Remy de Gourmont had most of the general intelligence of Aristotle. An amateur, though an excessively able amateur, in physiology, he combined to a remarkable degree sensitiveness, erudition, sense of fact and sense of history, and generalizing power.

We assume the gift of a superior sensibility. And for sensibility wide and profound reading does not mean merely a more extended pasture. There is not merely an increase of understanding, leaving the original acute impression unchanged. The new impressions modify the impressions received from the objects already known. An impression needs to be constantly refreshed by new impressions in order that it may persist at all; it needs to take its place in a system of impressions. And this system tends to become articulate in a generalized statement of literary beauty.

There are, for instance, many scattered lines and tercets in the *Divine Comedy* which are capable of transporting even a quite uninitiated reader, just sufficiently acquainted with the roots of the language to decipher the meaning, to an impression of over-powering beauty. This impression may be so deep that no subsequent study and understanding will intensify it. But at this point the impression is emotional; the reader in the ignorance which we postulate is unable to distinguish the poetry from an emotional state aroused in himself by the poetry, a state which may be merely an indulgence of his own emotions. The poetry may be an accidental stimulus. The end of the enjoyment of poetry is a pure contemplation from which all

the accidents of personal emotion are removed ;
thus we aim to see the object as it really is and
find a meaning for the words of Arnold. And
without a labour which is largely a labour of the
intelligence, we are unable to attain that stage
of vision *amor intellectualis Dei*.

Such considerations, cast in this general form,
may appear commonplaces. But I believe that it
is always opportune to call attention to the torpid
superstition that appreciation is one thing, and
" intellectual " criticism something else. Appreciation in popular psychology is one faculty, and
criticism another, an arid cleverness building
theoretical scaffolds upon one's own perceptions
or those of others. On the contrary, the true
generalization is not something superposed upon
an accumulation of perceptions ; the perceptions
do not, in a really appreciative mind, accumulate
as a mass, but form themselves as a structure ;
and criticism is the statement in language of this
structure ; it is a development of sensibility. The
bad criticism, on the other hand, is that which is
nothing but an expression of emotion. And
emotional people—such as stockbrokers, politicians,
men of science—and a few people who pride themselves on being unemotional—detest or applaud
great writers such as Spinoza or Stendhal because
of their " frigidity."

The writer of the present essay once committed
himself to the statement that " The poetic critic
is criticizing poetry in order to create poetry."

He is now inclined to believe that the " historical " and the " philosophical " critics had better be called historians and philosophers quite simply. As for the rest, there are merely various degrees of intelligence. It is fatuous to say that criticism is for the sake of " creation " or creation for the sake of criticism. It is also fatuous to assume that there are ages of criticism and ages of creativeness, as if by plunging ourselves into intellectual darkness we were in better hopes of finding spiritual light. The two directions of sensibility are complementary ; and as sensibility is rare, unpopular, and desirable, it is to be expected that the critic and the creative artist should frequently be the same person.

IMPERFECT CRITICS

SWINBURNE AS CRITIC

THREE conclusions at least issue from the perusal of Swinburne's critical essays : Swinburne had mastered his material, was more inward with the Tudor-Stuart dramatists than any man of pure letters before or since ; he is a more reliable guide to them than Hazlitt, Coleridge, or Lamb ; and his perception of relative values is almost always correct. Against these merits we may oppose two objections : the style is the prose style of Swinburne, and the content is not, in an exact sense, criticism. The faults of style are, of course, personal ; the tumultuous outcry of adjectives, the headstrong rush of undisciplined sentences, are the index to the impatience and perhaps laziness of a disorderly mind. But the style has one positive merit : it allows us to know that Swinburne was writing not to establish a critical reputation, not to instruct a docile public, but as a poet his notes upon poets whom he admired. And whatever our opinion of Swinburne's verse, the notes upon poets by a poet of Swinburne's dimensions must be read with attention and respect.

In saying that Swinburne's essays have the value

of notes of an important poet upon important
poets, we must place a check upon our expectancy.
He read everything, and he read with the single
interest in finding literature. The critics of the
romantic period were pioneers, and exhibit the
fallibility of discoverers. The selections of Lamb
are a successful effort of good taste, but anyone
who has referred to them after a thorough reading
of any of the poets included must have found that
some of the best passages—which must literally
have stared Lamb in the face—are omitted, while
sometimes others of less value are included. Hazlitt,
who committed himself to the judgment that the
Maid's Tragedy is one of the poorest of Beaumont
and Fletcher's plays, has no connected message to
deliver. Coleridge's remarks—too few and scattered—have permanent truth; but on some of
the greatest names he passes no remark, and of
some of the best plays was perhaps ignorant or
ill-informed. But compared with Swinburne, Coleridge writes much more as a poet might be expected
to write about poets. Of Massinger's verse Swinburne says :

It is more serviceable, more businesslike, more
eloquently practical, and more rhetorically effusive—
but never effusive beyond the bounds of effective
rhetoric—than the style of any Shakespearean or of
any Jonsonian dramatist.

It is impossible to tell whether Webster would
have found the style of Massinger more " service-

able " than his own for the last act of the *White Devil*, and indeed difficult to decide what " serviceable " here means ; but it is quite clear what Coleridge means when he says that Massinger's style

is much more easily constructed [than Shakespeare's], and may be more successfully adopted by writers in the present day.

Coleridge is writing as a professional with his eye on the technique. I do not know from what writing of Coleridge Swinburne draws the assertion that " Massinger often deals in exaggerated passion," but in the essay from which Swinburne quotes elsewhere Coleridge merely speaks of the " unnaturally irrational passions," a phrase much more defensible. Upon the whole, the two poets are in harmony upon the subject of Massinger ; and although Coleridge has said more in five pages, and said it more clearly, than Swinburne in thirty-nine, the essay of Swinburne is by no means otiose : it is more stimulating than Coleridge's, and the stimulation is never misleading. With all his superlatives, his judgment, if carefully scrutinized, appears temperate and just.

With all his justness of judgment, however, Swinburne is an appreciator and not a critic. In the whole range of literature covered, Swinburne makes hardly more than two judgments which can be reversed or even questioned : one, that Lyly is insignificant as a dramatist, and the other, that

Shirley was probably unaffected by Webster. The *Cardinal* is not a cast of the *Duchess of Malfi*, certainly ; but when Shirley wrote

> the mist is risen, and there's none
> To steer my wandering bark. (*Dies.*)

he was probably affected by

> My soul, like to a ship in a black storm,
> Is driven, I know not whither.

Swinburne's judgment is generally sound, his taste sensitive and discriminating. And we cannot say that his thinking is faulty or perverse—up to the point at which it is thinking. But Swinburne stops thinking just at the moment when we are most zealous to go on. And this arrest, while it does not vitiate his work, makes it an introduction rather than a statement.

We are aware, after the *Contemporaries of Shakespeare* and the *Age of Shakespeare* and the books on Shakespeare and Jonson, that there is something unsatisfactory in the way in which Swinburne was interested in these people ; we suspect that his interest was never articulately formulated in his mind or consciously directed to any purpose. He makes his way, or loses it, between two paths of definite direction. He might as a poet have concentrated his attention upon the technical problems solved or tackled by these men ; he might have traced for us the development of blank verse from Sackville to the mature Shakespeare, and its degeneration from Shakespeare to Milton. Or he might have studied through the literature to the mind of that century; he might, by dissection and analysis, have helped us to some insight into the feeling and thought which we seem to have left so far away. In either case, you would have had at least the excitement of following the movements of an important mind groping towards important conclusions. As it is, there are to be no conclusions, except that Elizabethan literature is very great, and that you can have pleasure and even ecstasy from it, because a sensitive poetic talent has had the experience. One is in risk of becoming fatigued by a hubbub that does not march; the drum is beaten, but the procession does not advance.

If, for example, Swinburne's interest was in poetry, why devote an essay to Brome? "The opening scene of the *Sparagus Garden*," says Swinburne, "is as happily humorous and as vividly natural as that of any more famous comedy." The scene is both humorous and natural. Brome deserves to be more read than he is, and first of all to be more accessible than he is. But Swinburne ought to suggest or imply (I do not say impose) a reason for reading the *Sparagus Garden* or the *Antipodes*, more sufficient than any he has provided. No doubt such reason could be found.

When it is a matter of pronouncing judgment between two poets, Swinburne is almost unerring. He is certainly right in putting Webster above Tourneur, Tourneur above Ford, and Ford above

Shirley. He weighs accurately the good and evil
in Fletcher : he perceives the essential theatricality,
but his comparison of the *Faithful Shepherdess* with
Comus is a judgment no word of which can be improved upon :

The difference between this poem [*i.e.* the *Faithful
Shepherdess*] and Milton's exquisitely imitative *Comus*
is the difference between a rose with a leaf or two faded
or falling, but still fragrant and radiant, and the fault-
less but scentless reproduction of a rose in academic
wax for the admiration and imitation of such craftsmen
as must confine their ambition to the laurels of a college
or the plaudits of a school.

In the longest and most important essay in the
Contemporaries of Shakespeare, the essay on Chapman, there are many such sentences of sound
judgment forcibly expressed. The essay is the
best we have on that great poet. It communicates
the sense of dignity and mass which we receive
from Chapman. But it also illustrates Swinburne's
infirmities. Swinburne was not tormented by
the restless desire to penetrate to the heart and
marrow of a poet, any more than he was tormented
by the desire to render the finest shades of difference
and resemblance between several poets. Chapman
is a difficult author, as Swinburne says ; he is far
more difficult than Jonson, to whom he bears only
a superficial likeness. He is difficult beyond his
obscurity. He is difficult partly through his pos-
session of a quality comparatively deficient in

Jonson, but which was nevertheless a quality of the age. It is strange that Swinburne should have hinted at a similarity to Jonson and not mentioned a far more striking affinity of Chapman's—that is, Donne. The man who wrote

> Guise, O my lord, how shall I cast from me
> The bands and coverts hindering me from thee ?
> The garment or the cover of the mind
> The humane soul is ; of the soul, the spirit
> The proper robe is ; of the spirit, the blood :
> And of the blood, the body is the shroud :

and

> Nothing is made of nought, of all things made,
> Their abstract being a dream but of a shade,

is unquestionably kin to Donne. The quality in question is not peculiar to Donne and Chapman. In common with the greatest—Marlowe, Webster, Tourneur, and Shakespeare—they had a quality of sensuous thought, or of thinking through the senses, or of the senses thinking, of which the exact formula remains to be defined. If you look for it in Shelley or Beddoes, both of whom in very different ways recaptured something of the Elizabethan inspiration, you will not find it, though you may find other qualities instead. There is a trace of it only in Keats, and, derived from a different source, in Rossetti. You will not find it in the *Duke of Gandia*. Swinburne's essay would have been all the better if he had applied himself to the solution of problems like this.

He did not apply himself to this sort of problem because this was not the sort of problem that interested him. The author of Swinburne's critical essays is also the author of Swinburne's verse : if you hold the opinion that Swinburne was a very great poet, you can hardly deny him the title of a great critic. There is the same curious mixture of qualities to produce Swinburne's own effect, resulting in the same blur, which only the vigour of the colours fixes. His great merit as a critic is really one which, like many signal virtues, can be stated so simply as to appear flat. It is that he was sufficiently interested in his subject-matter and knew quite enough about it ; and this is a rare combination in English criticism. Our critics are often interested in extracting something from their subject which is not fairly in it. And it is because this elementary virtue is so rare that Swinburne must take a very respectable place as a critic. Critics are often interested—but not quite in the nominal subject, often in something a little beside the point ; they are often learned— but not quite to the point either. (Swinburne knew some of the plays almost by heart.) Can this particular virtue at which we have glanced be attributed to Walter Pater ? or to Professor Bradley ? or to Swinburne's editor ?

A ROMANTIC ARISTOCRAT

It is impossible to overlook the merits of scholarship and criticism exhibited by George Wyndham's posthumous book, and it is impossible to deal with the book purely on its merits of scholarship and criticism. To attempt to do so would in the first place be unfair, as the book is a posthumous work, and posthumous books demand some personal attention to their writers. This book is a collection of essays and addresses, arranged in their present order by Mr. Whibley; they were intended by their author to be remodelled into a volume on "romantic literature"; they move from an ingenious search for the date of the beginning of Romanticism, through the French and English Renaissance, to Sir Walter Scott. In the second place, these essays represent the literary work of a man who gained his chief distinction in political life. In the third place, this man stands for a type, an English type. The type is interesting and will probably become extinct. It is natural, therefore, that our primary interest in the essays should be an interest in George Wyndham.

Mr. Charles Whibley, in an introduction the tone of which is well suited to the matter, has several sentences which throw light on Wyndham's personality. What issues with surprising clearness from Mr. Whibley's sketch is the unity of Wyndham's mind, the identity of his mind as it engaged in apparently unrelated occupations. Wyndham left Eton for the army; in barracks he "taught himself Italian, and filled his leisure with the reading of history and poetry." After this Coldstream culture there was a campaign in

Egypt ; later, service in South Africa accompanied
by a copy of Virgil. There was a career in the
Commons, a conspicuous career as Irish Secretary.
Finally, there was a career as a landowner—2400
acres. And throughout these careers George Wyndham went on not only accumulating books but
reading them, and occasionally writing about them.
He was a man of character, a man of energy. Mr.
Whibley is quite credible when he says :

Literature was for him no parergon, no mere way of
escape from politics. If he was an amateur in feeling,
he was a craftsman in execution ;

and, more significantly,

With the same zest that he read and discoursed upon
A Winter's Tale or *Troilus and Cressida*, he rode to
hounds, or threw himself with a kind of fury into a
" point to point," or made a speech at the hustings, or
sat late in the night talking with a friend.

From these and other sentences we chart the mind
of George Wyndham, and the key to its topography
is the fact that his literature and his politics and
his country life are one and the same thing. They
are not in separate compartments, they are one
career. Together they made up his world : literature, politics, riding to hounds. In the real world
these things have nothing to do with each other.
But we cannot believe that George Wyndham
lived in the real world. And this is implied in
Mr. Whibley's remark that ı

George Wyndham was by character and training a romantic. He looked with wonder upon the world as upon a fairyland.

Here is the manifestation of type.

There must probably be conceded to history a few " many-sided " men. Perhaps Leonardo da Vinci was such. George Wyndham was not a man on the scale of Leonardo, and his writings give a very different effect from Leonardo's notebooks. Leonardo turned to art or science, and each was what it was and not another thing. But Leonardo was Leonardo : he had no father to speak of, he was hardly a citizen, and he had no stake in the community. He lived in no fairyland, but his mind went out and became a part of things. George Wyndham was Gentry. He was chivalrous, the world was an adventure of himself. It is characteristic that on embarking as a subaltern for Egypt he wrote enthusiastically :

I do not suppose that any expedition since the days of Roman governors of provinces has started with such magnificence ; we might have been Antony going to Egypt in a purple-sailed galley.

This is precisely the spirit which animates his appreciation of the Elizabethans and of Walter Scott ; which guides him toward Hakluyt and North. Wyndham was enthusiastic, he was a Romantic, he was an Imperialist, and he was quite naturally a literary pupil of W. E. Henley. Wyndham was a scholar, but his scholarship is incidental ;

he was a good critic, within the range allowed him
by his enthusiasms ; but it is neither as Scholar
nor as Critic that we can criticize him. We can
criticize his writings only as the expression of this
peculiar English type, the aristocrat, the Imperialist,
the Romantic, riding to hounds across his prose,
looking with wonder upon the world as upon a
fairyland.

Because he belongs to this type, Wyndham wrote
enthusiastically and well about North's Plutarch.
The romance of the ancient world becomes more
romantic in the idiomatic prose of North ; the heroes
are not merely Greek and Roman heroes, but
Elizabethan heroes as well ; the romantic fusion
allured Wyndham. The charms of North could not
be expounded more delightfully, more seductively,
with more gusto, than they are in Wyndham's
essay. He appreciates the battles, the torchlight,
the " dead sound " of drums, the white, worn face
of Cicero in his flight peering from his litter ; he
appreciates the sharp brusque phrase of North :
" he roundly trussed them up and hung them by
their necks." And Wyndham is learned. Here,
as in his essays on the Pléiade and Shakespeare,
the man has read everything, with a labour that
only whets his enjoyment of the best. There
are two defects : a lack of balance and a lack of
critical profundity. The lack of balance peeps
through Wyndham's condemnation of an obviously
inferior translation of Plutarch : " He dedicated
the superfluity of his leisure to enjoyment, and

used his Lamia," says the bad translator.   North :
" he took pleasure of Lamia."   Wyndham makes a
set upon the bad translator.   But he forgets that
" dedicated the superfluity of his leisure " is such
a phrase as Gibbon would have warmed to life and
wit, and that a history, in the modern sense, could
not be written in the style of North.   Wyndham
forgets, in short, that it is not, in the end, periods
and traditions but individual men who write great
prose.   For Wyndham is himself a period and a
tradition.

The lack of balance is to be suspected elsewhere.
Wyndham *likes* the best, but he likes a good deal.
There is no conclusive evidence that he realized
all the difference, the gulf of difference between
lines like :

> En l'an trentiesme de mon aage
> Que toutes mes hontes j'ay beues ;

and even the very best of Ronsard or Bellay,
such as :

> Le temps s'en va, le temps s'en va, madame ;
> Las ! le temps, non, mais nous nous en allons
> Et tost serons estendus sous la lame.

We should not gather from Wyndham's essay that
the *Phœnix and Turtle* is a great poem, far finer
than *Venus and Adonis* ; but what he says about
Venus and Adonis is worth reading, for Wyndham
is very sharp in perceiving the neglected beauties
of the second-rate.   There is nothing to show the
gulf of difference between Shakespeare's sonnets

and those of any other Elizabethan. Wyndham
overrates Sidney, and in his references to Elizabethan writings on the theory of poetry omits
mention of the essay by Campion, an abler and more
daring though less common-sense study than
Daniel's. He speaks a few words for Drayton,
but has not noticed that the only good lines (with
the exception of one sonnet which may be an
accident) in Drayton's dreary sequence of " Ideas "
occur when Drayton drops his costume for a moment
and talks in terms of actuality :

> Lastly, mine eyes amazedly have seen
> Essex' great fall ; Tyrone his peace to gain ;
> The quiet end of that long-living queen ;
> The king's fair entry, and our peace with Spain.

More important than the lack of balance is the
lack of critical analysis. Wyndham had, as was
indicated, a gusto for the Elizabethans. His essay
on the Poems of Shakespeare contains an extraordinary amount of information. There is some
interesting gossip about Mary Fitton and a good
anecdote of Sir William Knollys. But Wyndham
misses what is the cardinal point in criticizing the
Elizabethans : we cannot grasp them, understand
them, without some understanding of the pathology
of rhetoric. Rhetoric, a particular form of rhetoric,
was endemic, it pervaded the whole organism ;
the healthy as well as the morbid tissues were
built up on it. We cannot grapple with even the
simplest and most conversational lines in Tudor

and early Stuart drama without having diagnosed
the rhetoric in the sixteenth- and seventeenth-
century mind. Even when we come across lines
like :

There's a plumber laying pipes in my guts, it scalds,

we must not allow ourselves to forget the rhetorical
basis any more than when we read :

Come, let us march against the powers of heaven
And set black streamers in the firmament
To signify the slaughter of the gods.

An understanding of Elizabethan rhetoric is as
essential to the appreciation of Elizabethan literature as an understanding of Victorian sentiment is
essential to the appreciation of Victorian literature and of George Wyndham.

Wyndham was a Romantic ; the only cure for
Romanticism is to analyse it. What is permanent
and good in Romanticism is curiosity—

. . . l' ardore
Ch' i' ebbe a divenir del mondo esperto
E degli vizii umani e del valore—

a curiosity which recognizes that any life, if accurately and profoundly penetrated, is interesting
and always strange. Romanticism is a short cut
to the strangeness without the reality, and it leads
its disciples only back upon themselves. George
Wyndham had curiosity, but he employed it
romantically, not to penetrate the real world, but
to complete the varied features of the world he

made for himself. It would be of interest to divagate from literature to politics and inquire to what extent Romanticism is incorporate in Imperialism ; to inquire to what extent Romanticism has possessed the imagination of Imperialists, and to what extent it was made use of by Disraeli. But this is quite another matter : there may be a good deal to be said for Romanticism in life, there is no place for it in letters. Not that we need conclude that a man of George Wyndham's antecedents and traditions must inevitably be a Romanticist writer. But this is the case when such a man plants himself firmly in his awareness of caste, when he says " The gentry must not abdicate." In politics this may be an admirable formula. It will not do in literature. The Arts insist that a man shall dispose of all that he has, even of his family tree, and follow art alone. For they require that a man be not a member of a family or of a caste or of a party or of a coterie, but simply and solely himself. A man like Wyndham brings several virtues into literature. But there is only one man better and more uncommon than the patrician, and that is the Individual.

The Local Flavour

In a world which is chiefly occupied with the task of keeping up to date with itself, it is a satisfaction to know that there is at least one man who has not only read but enjoyed, and not only enjoyed but read, such authors as Petronius and Herondas.

That is Mr. Charles Whibley, and there are two statements to make about him : that he is not a critic, and that he is something which is almost as rare, if not quite as precious. He has apparently read and enjoyed a great deal of English literature, and the part of it that he has most enjoyed is the literature of the great ages, the sixteenth and seventeenth centuries. We may opine that Mr. Whibley has not uttered a single important original judgment upon any of this literature. On the other hand, how many have done so ? Mr. Whibley is not a critic of men or of books ; but he convinces us that if we read the books that he has read we should find them as delightful as he has found them ; and if we read them we can form our own opinions. And if he has not the balance of the critic, he has some other equipoise of his own. It is partly that his tastes are not puritanical, that he can talk about Restoration dramatists and others without apologizing for their " indecency " ; it is partly his sense for the best local and temporal flavours ; it is partly his healthy appetite.

A combination of non-critical, rather than uncritical, qualities made Mr. Whibley the most appropriate person in the world for the work by which he is best known. We should be more grateful for the " Tudor Translations Series " if we could find copies to be bought, and if we could afford to buy them when we found them. But that is not Mr. Whibley's fault. The introductions which he wrote for some of the translators are all that such introductions should be.   His Urquhart's *Rabelais* contains all the irrelevant information about that writer which is what is wanted to stimulate a taste for him.   After reading the introduction, to read Urquhart was the only pleasure in life.   And therefore, in a country destitute of living criticism, Mr. Whibley is a useful person : for the first thing is that English literature should be read at all.   The few people who talk intelligently about Stendhal and Flaubert and James know this ; but the large number of people who skim the conversation of the former do not know enough of English literature to be even insular.   There are two ways in which a writer may lead us to profit by the work of dead writers.   One is by isolating the essential, by pointing out the most intense in various kinds and separating it from the accidents of environment.   This method is helpful only to the more intelligent people, who are capable of a unique enjoyment of perfect expression, and it concentrates on the very best in any art.   The other method, that of Mr. Whibley, is to communicate a taste for the period—and for the best of the period so far as it is of that period.   That is not very easy either.   For a pure journalist will not know any period well enough ; a pure dilettante will know it too egotistically, as a fashion of his own.   Mr. Whibley is really interested ; and he has escaped, without any programme of revolt, from the present century into those of Tudor and Stuart.   He escapes, and perhaps leads others, by virtue of a taste which is not exactly a literary taste.

The "Tudor Translations" form part of a pronounced taste. Some are better written than others. There is, of course, a world of difference —of which Mr. Whibley is perhaps unaware— between even Florio and his original. The French of Montaigne is a mature language, and the English of Florio's living translation is not. Montaigne could be translated into the English of his time, but a similar work could not have been written in it. But as the English language matured it lost something that Florio and all his inferior colleagues had, and that they had in common with the language of Montaigne. It was not only the language, but the time. The prose of that age had life, a life to which later ages could not add, from which they could only take away. You find the same life, the same abundance, in Montaigne and Brantôme, the alteration in Rochefoucauld as in Hobbes, the desiccation in the classic prose of both languages, in Voltaire and in Gibbon. Only, the French was originally richer and more mature—already in Joinville and Commines—and we have no prose to compare with Montaigne and Rabelais. If Mr. Whibley had analysed this vitality, and told us why Holland and Underdowne, Nashe and Martin Marprelate are still worth reading, then he could have shown us how to recognize this quality when it, or something like it, appears in our own lifetime. But Mr.

Whibley is not an analyst. His taste, even, becomes less certain as he fixes it on individuals within his period. On Surrey's blank verse he is feeble ; he does not even give Surrey the credit of having anticipated some of Tennyson's best effects. He has no praise for Golding, quite one of the best of the verse translators ; he apologizes for him by saying that Ovid demands no strength or energy ! There is strength and energy, at least, in Marlowe's *Amores*. And he omits mention of Gawain Douglas, who, though he wrote in Scots, was surely a " Tudor " translator. Characteristically, Mr. Whibley praises Chapman because

it gives proof of an abounding life, a quenchless energy. There is a grandeur and spirit in Chapman's rendering, not unworthy the original . . .

This is commonplace, and it is uncritical. And a critic would not use so careless a phrase as " Tasso's masterpiece." The essay on Congreve does not add much to our understanding :

And so he set upon the boards a set of men and women of quick brains and cynical humours, who talked with the brilliance and rapidity wherewith the finished swordsman fences.

We have heard of this conversation like fencing before. And the suspicion is in our breast that Mr. Whibley might admire George Meredith. The essay on Ralegh gives still less. The reality of that pleasing pirate and monopolist has escaped, and only the national hero is left.   And yet Ralegh, and Swift, and Congreve, and the underworld of sixteenth and seventeenth-century letters, are somehow kept alive by what Mr. Whibley says of them.

Accordingly, Mr. Whibley does not disappear in the jungle of journalism and false criticism ; he deserves a " place upon the shelves " of those who care for English literature.   He has the first requisite of a critic : interest in his subject, and ability to communicate an interest in it.   His defects are both of intellect and feeling.   He has no dissociative faculty.   There were very definite vices and definite shortcomings and immaturities in the literature he admires ; and as he is not the person to tell us of the vices and shortcomings, he is not the person to lay before us the work of absolutely the finest quality.   He exercises neither of the tools of the critic : comparison and analysis.   He has not the austerity of passion which can detect unerringly the transition from work of eternal intensity to work that is merely beautiful, and from work that is beautiful to work that is merely charming.   For the critic needs to be able not only to saturate himself in the spirit and the fashion of a time—the local flavour—but also to separate himself suddenly from it in appreciation of the highest creative work.

And he needs something else that Mr. Whibley lacks : a creative interest, a focus upon the immediate future.   The important critic is the person who is absorbed in the present problems of art, and who wishes to bring the forces of the past to bear upon the solution of these problems. If the critic consider Congreve, for instance, he will have always at the back of his mind the question : What has Congreve got that is pertinent to our dramatic art ? Even if he is solely engaged in trying to understand Congreve, this will make all the difference ; inasmuch as to understand anything is to understand from a point of view. Most critics have some creative interest—it may be, instead of an interest in any art, an interest (like Mr. Paul More's) in morals. These remarks were introduced only to assist in giving the books of Mr. Whibley a place, a particular but unticketed place, neither with criticism, nor with history, nor with plain journalism ; and the trouble would not have been taken if the books were not thought to be worth placing.

A Note on the American Critic

This gallery of critics is not intended to be in any sense complete. But having dealt with three English writers of what may be called critical prose, one's mind becomes conscious of the fact that they have something in common, and, trying to perceive more clearly what this community is, and suspecting that it is a national quality, one is impelled to meditate upon the strongest contrast possible. Hence these comments upon two American critics and one French critic, which would not take exactly this form without the contrast at which I have hinted.

Mr. Paul More is the author of a number of volumes which he perhaps hopes will break the record of mass established by the complete works of Sainte-Beuve. The comparison with Sainte-Beuve is by no means trivial, for Mr. More, and Professor Irving Babbitt also, are admirers of the voluminous Frenchman. Not only are they admirers, but their admiration is perhaps a clue both to much of their merit and to some of their defects. In the first place, both of these writers have given much more attention to French criticism, to the study of French standards of writing and of thought, than any of the notable English critics since Arnold; they are therefore much nearer to the European current, although they exhibit faults which are definitely transatlantic and which definitely keep them out of it. The French influence is traceable in their devotion to ideas and their interest in problems of art and life as problems which exist and can be handled apart from their relations to the critic's private temperament. With Swinburne, the criticism of Elizabethan literature has the interest of a passion, it has the interest for us of any writing by an intellectual man who is genuinely moved by certain poetry. Swinburne's intelligence is not defective, it is impure. There are few ideas in Swinburne's critical writings which stand forth luminous with an independent life of their own, so true that one forgets the author in the statement. Swinburne's words must always be referred back to Swinburne himself. And if literature is to Swinburne merely a passion, we are tempted to say that to George Wyndham it was a hobby, and to Mr. Whibley almost a charming show-man's show (we are charmed by the urbanity of the showman). The two latter have gusto, but gusto is no equivalent for taste ; it depends too much upon the appetite and the digestion of the feeder. And with one or two other writers, whom I have not had occasion to discuss, literature is not so much a col-lection of valuable porcelain as an institution—accepted, that is to say, with the same gravity as the establishments of Church and State. That is, in other words, the essentially uncritical attitude. In all of these attitudes the English critic is the victim of his temperament. He may acquire great erudi-tion, but erudition easily becomes a hobby ; it is useless unless it enables us to see literature all round, to detach it from ourselves, to reach a state of pure contemplation.

Now Mr. More and Mr. Babbitt have endeavoured to establish a criticism which should be independent of temperament. This is in itself a considerable merit. But at this point Mr. More particularly has been led astray, oddly enough, by his guide Sainte-Beuve. Neither Mr. More nor Sainte-Beuve is primarily interested in art. Of the latter M. Benda has well observed that

on sait—et c'est certainement un des grands éléments de son succès—combien d'études l'illustre critique con-sacre à des auteurs dont l'importance littéraire est quasi nulle (femmes, magistrats, courtisans, militaires), mais dont les écrits lui sont une occasion de pourtraiturer une âme ; combien volontiers, pour les maîtres, il s'attache à leurs productions secondaires, notes, brouillons, lettres intimes, plutôt qu'à leurs grandes œuvres, souvent beaucoup moins expressives, en effet, de leur psychologie.

Mr. More is not, like Sainte-Beuve, primarily interested in psychology or in human beings ; Mr. More is primarily a moralist, which is a worthy and serious thing to be. The trouble with Mr. More is that you cannot disperse a theory or point of view of morals over a vast number of essays on a great variety of important figures in literature, unless you can give some more particular interest as well. Sainte-Beuve has his particularized interest in human beings ; another critic—say Remy de Gourmont— may have something to say always about the art of a writer which will make our enjoyment of that writer more conscious and more intelligent. But the pure moralist in letters—the moralist is useful to the creator as well as the reader of poetry—must be more concise, for we must have the pleasure of inspecting the beauty of his structure. And here M. Julien Benda has a great advantage over Mr. More ; his thought may be less profound, but it has more formal beauty.

Mr. Irving Babbitt, who shares so many of the ideals and opinions of Mr. More that their names must be coupled, has expressed his thought more abstractly and with more form, and is free from a mystical impulse which occasionally gets out of Mr. More's hand. He appears, more clearly than Mr.

More, and certainly more clearly than any critic of
equal authority in America or England, to perceive
Europe as a whole ; he has the cosmopolitan mind
and a tendency to seek the centre. His few books
are important, and would be more important if he
preached of discipline in a more disciplined style.
Although he also is an admirer of Sainte-Beuve, he
would probably subscribe to this admirable paragraph of Othenin d'Haussonville : [1]

Il y a une beauté littéraire, impersonnelle en quelque
sorte, parfaitement distincte de l'auteur lui-même et
de son organisation, beauté qui a sa raison d'être et
ses lois, dont la critique est tenue de rendre compte.
Et si la critique considère cette tâche comme au-dessous
d'elle, si c'est affaire à la rhétorique et à ce que Sainte-
Beuve appelle dédaigneusement les Quintilien, alors la
rhétorique a du bon et les Quintilien ne sont pas à
dédaigner.

There may be several critics in England who would
applaud this notion ; there are very few who show
any evidence of its apprehension in their writings.
But Mr. More and Mr. Babbitt, whatever their actual
tastes, and although they are not primarily occupied
with art, are on the side of the artist. And the side
of the artist is not the side which in England is often
associated with critical writing. As Mr. More has
pointed out in an interesting essay, there is a vital
weakness in Arnold's definition of criticism as " the

[1] *Revue des Deux Mondes*, fevr. 1875, quoted by Benda,
Belphégor, p. 140.

disinterested endeavour to know the best that is known and thought in the world, irrespectively of practice, politics, and everything of the kind." The " disinterested endeavour to know " is only a pre-requisite of the *critic*, and is not *criticism*, which may be the result of such an endeavour. Arnold states the work of the critic merely in terms of the personal ideal, an ideal for oneself—and an ideal for oneself is not disinterested. Here Arnold is the Briton rather than the European.

Mr. More indicates his own attitude in praising those whom he elevates to the position of masters of criticism :

If they deal much with the criticism of literature, this is because in literature more manifestly than anywhere else life displays its infinitely varied motives and results ; and their practice is always to render literature itself more consciously a criticism of life.

" Criticism of life " is a facile phrase, and at most only represents one aspect of great literature, if it does not assign to the term " criticism " itself a generality which robs it of precision. Mr. More has, it seems to me, in this sentence just failed to put his finger on the right seriousness of great literary art ; the seriousness which we find in Villon's *Testament* and which is conspicuously absent from *In Memoriam* ; or the seriousness which controls *Amos Barton* and not *The Mill on the Floss*.

It is a pity that Mr. More does not write a little oftener about the great literary artists, it is a pity that he takes the reputations of the world too solemnly. This is probably due in part to remoteness in space from the European centre. But it must be observed that English solemnity and American solemnity are very different. I do not propose to analyse the difference (it would be a valuable chapter in social history) ; the American solemnity, it is enough to say, is more primitive, more academic, more like that of the German professor. But it is not the fault of Mr. More or Mr. Babbitt that the culture of ideas has only been able to survive in America in the unfavourable atmosphere of the university.

THE FRENCH INTELLIGENCE

As the inspection of types of English irresistibly provoked a glance at two American critics, so the inspection of the latter leads our attention to the French. M. Julien Benda has the formal beauty which the American critics lack, and a close affinity to them in point of view. He restricts himself, perhaps, to a narrower field of ideas, but within that field he manipulates the ideas with a very exceptional cogency and clarity. To notice his last book (*Belphégor : essai sur l'esthétique de la présente société française*) would be to quote from it. M. Benda is not like Remy de Gourmont, the critical consciousness of a generation, he could not supply the conscious formulas of a sensibility in process of formation ; he is rather the ideal scavenger of the rubbish of our time. Much of his analysis of the decadence of contemporary French society could be applied to London, although differences are observable from his diagnosis.

Quant à la société en elle-même, on peut prévoir que ce soin qu'elle met à éprouver de l'émoi par l'art, devenant cause à son tour, y rendra la soif de ce plaisir de plus en plus intense, l'application à la satisfaire de plus en plus jalouse et plus perfectionnée. On entrevoit le jour où la bonne société française repudiera encore le peu qu'elle supporte aujourd'hui d'idées et d'organisation dans l'art, et ne se passionera plus que pour des gestes de comédiens, pour des impressions de femmes ou d'enfants, pour des rugissements de lyriques, pour des extases de fanatiques. . . .

Almost the only person who has ever figured in England and attempted a task at all similar to that of M. Benda is Matthew Arnold. Matthew Arnold was intelligent, and by so much difference as the presence of one intelligent man makes, our age is inferior to that of Arnold. But what an advantage a man like M. Benda has over Arnold. It is not simply that he has a critical tradition behind him, and that Arnold is using a language which constantly tempts the user away from dispassionate exposition into sarcasm and diatribe, a language less fitted for criticism than the English of the eighteenth century. It is that the follies and stupidities of the French, no matter how base, express themselves in the form of ideas—Bergsonism itself is an intellectual construction, and the mondaines who attended lectures at the College de France were in a sense using their

3

minds. A man of ideas needs ideas, or pseudo-ideas, to fight against. And Arnold lacked the active resistance which is necessary to keep a mind at its sharpest.

A society in which a mind like M. Benda's can exercise itself, and in which there are persons like M. Benda, is one which facilitates the task of the creative artist. M. Benda cannot be attached, like Gourmont, to any creative group. He does not wholly partake in that "conscious creation of the field of the present out of the past" which Mr. More considers to be part of the work of the critic. But in analysing the maladies of the second-rate or corrupt literature of the time he makes the labour of the creative artist lighter. The Charles Louis Philippes of English literature are never done with, because there is no one to kill their reputations ; we still hear that George Meredith is a master of prose, or even a profound philosopher. The creative artist in England finds himself compelled, or at least tempted, to spend much of his time and energy in criticism that he might reserve for the perfecting of his proper work : simply because there is no one else to do it.

TRADITION AND THE INDIVIDUAL TALENT

I

IN English writing we seldom speak of tradition, though we occasionally apply its name in deploring its absence. We cannot refer to " the tradition " or to " a tradition " ; at most, we employ the adjective in saying that the poetry of So-and-so is " traditional " or even " too traditional." Seldom, perhaps, does the word appear except in a phrase of censure. If otherwise, it is vaguely approbative, with the implication, as to the work approved, of some pleasing archæological reconstruction. You can hardly make the word agreeable to English ears without this comfortable reference to the reassuring science of archæology.

Certainly the word is not likely to appear in our appreciations of living or dead writers. Every nation, every race, has not only its own creative, but its own critical turn of mind ; and is even more oblivious of the shortcomings and limitations of its critical habits than of those of its creative genius. We know, or think we know, from the enormous mass of critical writing that has appeared in the French

language the critical method or habit of the French ;
we only conclude (we are such unconscious people)
that the French are " more critical " than we, and
sometimes even plume ourselves a little with the
fact, as if the French were the less spontaneous.
Perhaps they are ; but we might remind ourselves
that criticism is as inevitable as breathing, and that
we should be none the worse for articulating what
passes in our minds when we read a book and feel
an emotion about it, for criticizing our own minds in
their work of criticism.   One of the facts that might
come to light in this process is our tendency to insist,
when we praise a poet, upon those aspects of his
work in which he least resembles anyone else.   In
these aspects or parts of his work we pretend to find
what is individual, what is the peculiar essence of
the man.   We dwell with satisfaction upon the poet's
difference from his predecessors, especially his immediate predecessors ; we endeavour to find something
that can be isolated in order to be enjoyed.   Whereas if we approach a poet without his prejudice we
shall often find that not only the best, but the most
individual parts of his work may be those in which
the dead poets, his ancestors, assert their immortality
most vigorously.   And I do not mean the impression-
able period of adolescence, but the period of full
maturity.

Yet if the only form of tradition, of handing down,
consisted in following the ways of the immediate
generation before us in a blind or timid adherence to
its successes, " tradition " should positively be dis-

couraged. We have seen many such simple currents soon lost in the sand ; and novelty is better than repetition. Tradition is a matter of much wider significance. It cannot be inherited, and if you want it you must obtain it by great labour. It involves, in the first place, the historical sense, which we may call nearly indispensable to anyone who would continue to be a poet beyond his twenty-fifth year ; and the historical sense involves a perception, not only of the pastness of the past, but of its presence ; the historical sense compels a man to write not merely with his own generation in his bones, but with a feeling that the whole of the literature of Europe from Homer and within it the whole of the literature of his own country has a simultaneous existence and composes a simultaneous order. This historical sense, which is a sense of the timeless as well as of the temporal and of the timeless and of the temporal together, is what makes a writer traditional. And it is at the same time what makes a writer most acutely conscious of his place in time, of his contemporaneity.

No poet, no artist of any art, has his complete meaning alone. His significance, his appreciation is the appreciation of his relation to the dead poets and artists. You cannot value him alone ; you must set him, for contrast and comparison, among the dead. I mean this as a principle of æsthetic, not merely historical, criticism. The necessity that he shall conform, that he shall cohere, is not one-sided ; what happens when a new work of art is created is something that happens simultaneously to all the works of art which preceded it. The existing monuments form an ideal order among themselves, which is modified by the introduction of the new (the really new) work of art among them. The existing order is complete before the new work arrives ; for order to persist after the supervention of novelty, the *whole* existing order must be, if ever so slightly, altered ; and so the relations, proportions, values of each work of art toward the whole are readjusted ; and this is conformity between the old and the new. Whoever has approved this idea of order, of the form of European, of English literature, will not find it preposterous that the past should be altered by the present as much as the present is directed by the past. And the poet who is aware of this will be aware of great difficulties and responsibilities.

In a peculiar sense he will be aware also that he must inevitably be judged by the standards of the past. I say judged, not amputated, by them ; not judged to be as good as, or worse or better than, the dead ; and certainly not judged by the canons of dead critics. It is a judgment, a comparison, in which two things are measured by each other. To conform merely would be for the new work not really to conform at all ; it would not be new, and would therefore not be a work of art. And we do not quite say that the new is more valuable because it fits in ; but its fitting in is a test of its value—a test, it is true, which can only be slowly and cautiously applied, for we are none of us infallible judges of conformity. We say : it appears to conform, and is perhaps individual, or it appears individual, and may conform ; but we are hardly likely to find that it is one and not the other.

To proceed to a more intelligible exposition of the relation of the poet to the past : he can neither take the past as a lump, an indiscriminate bolus, nor can he form himself wholly on one or two private admirations, nor can he form himself wholly upon one preferred period. The first course is inadmissible, the second is an important experience of youth, and the third is a pleasant and highly desirable supplement. The poet must be very conscious of the main current, which does not at all flow invariably through the most distinguished reputations. He must be quite aware of the obvious fact that art never improves, but that the material of art is never quite the same. He must be aware that the mind of Europe—the mind of his own country—a mind which he learns in time to be much more important than his own private mind—is a mind which changes, and that this change is a development which abandons nothing *en route*, which does not superannuate either Shakespeare, or Homer, or the rock drawing of the Magdalenian draughtsmen. That this development, refinement perhaps, complication certainly, is not, from the point of view of the artist, any improvement. Perhaps not even an improvement from the point of view of the psychologist or not to the extent which we imagine ; perhaps only in the end based upon a complication in economics and machinery. But the difference between the present and the past is that the conscious present is an awareness of the past in a way and to an extent which the past's awareness of itself cannot show.

Some one said: " The dead writers are remote from us because we *know* so much more than they did." Precisely, and they are that which we know.

I am alive to a usual objection to what is clearly part of my programme for the *métier* of poetry. The objection is that the doctrine requires a ridiculous amount of erudition (pedantry), a claim which can be rejected by appeal to the lives of poets in any pantheon. It will even be affirmed that much learning deadens or perverts poetic sensibility. While, however, we persist in believing that a poet ought to know as much as will not encroach upon his necessary receptivity and necessary laziness, it is not desirable to confine knowledge to whatever can be put into a useful shape for examinations, drawing-rooms, or the still more pretentious modes of publicity. Some can absorb knowledge, the more tardy must sweat for it. Shakespeare acquired more essential history from Plutarch than most men could from the whole British Museum. What is to be insisted upon is that the poet must develop or procure the consciousness of the past and that he should continue to develop this consciousness throughout his career.

What happens is a continual surrender of himself as he is at the moment to something which is more valuable. The progress of an artist is a continual self-sacrifice, a continual extinction of personality.

There remains to define this process of depersonalization and its relation to the sense of tradition. It is in this depersonalization that art may be said to approach the condition of science. I shall, therefore, invite you to consider, as a suggestive analogy, the action which takes place when a bit of finely filiated platinum is introduced into a chamber containing oxygen and sulphur dioxide.

II

Honest criticism and sensitive appreciation is directed not upon the poet but upon the poetry. If we attend to the confused cries of the newspaper critics and the susurrus of popular repetition that follows, we shall hear the names of poets in great numbers ; if we seek not Blue-book knowledge but the enjoyment of poetry, and ask for a poem, we shall seldom find it. In the last article I tried to point out the importance of the relation of the poem to other poems by other authors, and suggested the conception of poetry as a living whole of all the poetry that has ever been written. The other aspect of this Impersonal theory of poetry is the relation of the poem to its author. And I hinted, by an analogy, that the mind of the mature poet differs from that of the immature one not precisely in any valuation of " personality," not being necessarily more interesting, or having " more to say," but rather by being a more finely perfected medium in which special, or very varied, feelings are at liberty to enter into new combinations.

The analogy was that of the catalyst. When the two gases previously mentioned are mixed in the presence of a filament of platinum, they form sulphurous acid. This combination takes place only if the platinum is present ; nevertheless the newly formed acid contains no trace of platinum, and the platinum itself is apparently unaffected ; has remained inert, neutral, and unchanged. The mind of the poet is the shred of platinum. It may partly or exclusively operate upon the experience of the man himself ; but, the more perfect the artist, the more completely separate in him will be the man who suffers and the mind which creates ; the more perfectly will the mind digest and transmute the passions which are its material.

The experience, you will notice, the elements which enter the presence of the transforming catalyst, are of two kinds : emotions and feelings. The effect of a work of art upon the person who enjoys it is an experience different in kind from any experience not of art. It may be formed out of one emotion, or may be a combination of several ; and various feelings, inhering for the writer in particular words or phrases or images, may be added to compose the final result. Or great poetry may be made without the direct use of any emotion whatever : composed out of feelings solely. Canto XV of the *Inferno* (Brunetto Latini) is a working up of the emotion evident in the situation ; but the effect, though single as that of any work of art, is obtained by considerable complexity of detail. The last quatrain gives an image, a feeling attaching to an image, which " came," which did not develop simply out of what precedes, but which was probably in suspension in the poet's mind until the proper combination arrived for it to add itself to. The poet's mind is in fact a receptacle for seizing and storing up numberless feelings, phrases, images, which remain there until all the particles which can unite to form a new compound are present together.

If you compare several representative passages of the greatest poetry you see how great is the variety of types of combination, and also how completely any semi-ethical criterion of " sublimity " misses the mark. For it is not the " greatness," the intensity, of the emotions, the components, but the intensity of the artistic process, the pressure, so to speak, under which the fusion takes place, that counts. The episode of Paolo and Francesca employs a definite emotion, but the intensity of the poetry is something quite different from whatever intensity in the supposed experience it may give the impression of. It is no more intense, furthermore, than Canto XXVI, the voyage of Ulysses, which has not the direct dependence upon an emotion. Great variety is possible in the process of transmution of emotion : the murder of Agamemnon, or the agony of Othello, gives an artistic effect apparently closer to a possible original than the scenes from Dante. In the *Agamemnon*, the artistic emotion approxi-

mates to the emotion of an actual spectator ; in
Othello to the emotion of the protagonist himself.
But the difference between art and the event is
always absolute ; the combination which is the
murder of Agamemnon is probably as complex as
that which is the voyage of Ulysses. In either case
there has been a fusion of elements. The ode of
Keats contains a number of feelings which have
nothing particular to do with the nightingale, but
which the nightingale, partly, perhaps, because of
its attractive name, and partly because of its reputation, served to bring together.

The point of view which I am struggling to attack
is perhaps related to the metaphysical theory of the
substantial unity of the soul : for my meaning is,
that the poet has, not a " personality " to express,
but a particular medium, which is only a medium
and not a personality, in which impressions and
experiences combine in peculiar and unexpected
ways. Impressions and experiences which are important for the man may take no place in the poetry,
and those which become important in the poetry
may play quite a negligible part in the man, the
personality.

I will quote a passage which is unfamiliar enough
to be regarded with fresh attention in the light—or
darkness—of these observations :

> And now methinks I could e'en chide myself
> For doating on her beauty, though her death
> Shall be revenged after no common action.
> Does the silkworm expend her yellow labours

> For thee ? For thee does she undo herself ?
> Are lordships sold to maintain ladyships
> For the poor benefit of a bewildering minute ?
> Why does yon fellow falsify highways,
> And put his life between the judge's lips,
> To refine such a thing—keeps horse and men
> To beat their valours for her ? . . .

In this passage (as is evident if it is taken in its context) there is a combination of positive and negative emotions : an intensely strong attraction toward beauty and an equally intense fascination by the ugliness which is contrasted with it and which destroys it. This balance of contrasted emotion is in the dramatic situation to which the speech is pertinent, but that situation alone is inadequate to it. This is, so to speak, the structural emotion, provided by the drama. But the whole effect, the dominant tone, is due to the fact that a number of floating feelings, having an affinity to this emotion by no means superficially evident, have combined with it to give us a new art emotion.

It is not in his personal emotions, the emotions provoked by particular events in his life, that the poet is in any way remarkable or interesting. His particular emotions may be simple, or crude, or flat. The emotion in his poetry will be a very complex thing, but not with the complexity of the emotions of people who have very complex or unusual emotions in life. One error, in fact, of eccentricity in poetry is to seek for new human emotions to express ; and in this search for novelty in the wrong place it discovers the perverse. The business of the poet is not to find new emotions, but to use the ordinary ones and, in working them up into poetry, to express feelings which are not in actual emotions at all. And emotions which he has never experienced will serve his turn as well as those familiar to him. Consequently, we must believe that " emotion recollected in tranquillity " is an inexact formula. For it is neither emotion, nor recollection, nor, without distortion of meaning, tranquillity. It is a concentration, and a new thing resulting from the concentration, of a very great number of experiences which to the practical and active person would not seem to be experiences at all ; it is a concentration which does not happen consciously or of deliberation. These experiences are not " recollected," and they finally unite in an atmosphere which is " tranquil " only in that it is a passive attending upon the event. Of course this is not quite the whole story. There is a great deal, in the writing of poetry, which must be conscious and deliberate. In fact, the bad poet is usually unconscious where he ought to be conscious, and conscious where he ought to be unconscious. Both errors tend to make him " personal." Poetry is not a turning loose of emotion, but an escape from emotion ; it is not the expression of personality, but an escape from personality. But, of course, only those who have personality and emotions know what it means to want to escape from these things.

III

ὁ δὲ νοῦς ἴσως θειότερόν τι καὶ ἀπαθές ἐστιν

This essay proposes to halt at the frontier of metaphysics or mysticism, and confine itself to such practical conclusions as can be applied by the responsible person interested in poetry. To divert interest from the poet to the poetry is a laudable aim : for it would conduce to a juster estimation of actual poetry, good and bad. There are many people who appreciate the expression of sincere emotion in verse, and there is a smaller number of people who can appreciate technical excellence. But very few know when there is expression of *significant* emotion, emotion which has its life in the poem and not in the history of the poet. The emotion of art is impersonal. And the poet cannot reach this impersonality without surrendering himself wholly to the work to be done. And he is not likely to know what is to be done unless he lives in what is not merely the present, but the present moment of the past, unless he is conscious, not of what is dead, but of what is already living.

THE POSSIBILITY OF A POETIC DRAMA

THE questions—why there is no poetic drama to-day, how the stage has lost all hold on literary art, why so many poetic plays are written which can only be read, and read, if at all, without pleasure—have become insipid, almost academic. The usual conclusion is either that " conditions " are too much for us, or that we really prefer other types of literature, or simply that we are uninspired. As for the last alternative, it is not to be entertained ; as for the second, what type do we prefer ? ; and as for the first, no one has ever shown me " conditions," except of the most superficial. The reasons for raising the question again are first that the majority, perhaps, certainly a large number, of poets hanker for the stage ; and second, that a not negligible public appears to want verse plays. Surely there is some legitimate craving, not restricted to a few persons, which only the verse play can satisfy. And surely the critical attitude is to attempt to analyse the conditions and the other data. If there comes to light some conclusive obstacle, the investigation should at least help us to turn our thoughts to more profitable pursuits ;

and if there is not, we may hope to arrive eventually at some statement of conditions which might be altered. Possibly we shall find that our incapacity has a deeper source : the arts have at times flourished when there was no drama ; possibly we are incompetent altogether ; in that case the stage will be, not the seat, but at all events a symptom, of the malady.

From the point of view of literature, the drama is only one among several poetic forms. The epic, the ballad, the chanson de geste, the forms of Provence and of Tuscany, all found their perfection by serving particular societies. The forms of Ovid, Catullus, Propertius, served a society different, and in some respects more civilized, than any of these ; and in the society of Ovid the drama as a form of art was comparatively insignificant. Nevertheless, the drama is perhaps the most permanent, is capable of greater variation and of expressing more varied types of society, than any other. It varied considerably in England alone ; but when one day it was discovered lifeless, subsequent forms which had enjoyed a transitory life were dead too. I am not prepared to undertake the historical survey ; but I should say that the poetic drama's autopsy was performed as much by Charles Lamb as by anyone else. For a form is not wholly dead until it is known to be ; and Lamb, by exhuming the remains of dramatic life at its fullest, brought a consciousness of the immense gap between present and past. It was impossible to believe, after that, in a dramatic

" tradition." The relation of Byron's *English Bards* and the poems of Crabbe to the work of Pope was a continuous tradition ; but the relation of *The Cenci* to the great English drama is almost that of a reconstruction to an original. By losing tradition, we lose our hold on the present ; but so far as there was any dramatic tradition in Shelley's day there was nothing worth the keeping. There is all the difference between perservation and restoration.

The Elizabethan Age in England was able to absorb a great quantity of new thoughts and new images, almost dispensing with tradition, because it had this great form of its own which imposed itself on everything that came to it. Consequently, the blank verse of their plays accomplished a subtlety and consciousness, even an intellectual power, that no blank verse since has developed or even repeated ; elsewhere this age is crude, pedantic, or loutish in comparison with its contemporary France or Italy. The nineteenth century had a good many fresh impressions ; but it had no form in which to confine them. Two men, Wordsworth and Browning, hammered out forms for themselves—personal forms, *The Excursion, Sordello, The Ring and the Book, Dramatic Monologues* ; but no man can invent a form, create a taste for it, and perfect it too. Tennyson, who might unquestionably have been a consummate master of minor forms, took to turning out large patterns on a machine. As for Keats and Shelley, they were too young to be judged, and they were trying one form after another.

These poets were certainly obliged to consume vast energy in this pursuit of form, which could never lead to a wholly satisfying result. There has only been one Dante ; and, after all, Dante had the benefit of years of practice in forms employed and altered by numbers of contemporaries and predecessors ; he did not waste the years of youth in metric invention ; and when he came to the *Commedia* he knew how to pillage right and left. To have, given into one's hands, a crude form, capable of indefinite refinement, and to be the person to see the possibilities—Shakespeare was very fortunate. And it is perhaps the craving for some such *donnée* which draws us on toward the present mirage of poetic drama.

But it is now very questionable whether there are more than two or three in the present generation who are *capable*, the least little bit, of benefiting by such advantages were they given. At most two or three actually devote themselves to this pursuit of form for which they have little or no public recognition. To create a form is not merely to invent a shape, a rhyme or rhythm. It is also the realization of the whole appropriate content of this rhyme or rhythm. The sonnet of Shakespeare is not merely such and such a pattern, but a precise way of thinking and feeling. The *framework* which was provided for the Elizabethan dramatist was not merely blank verse and the five-act play and the Elizabethan playhouse ; it was not merely the plot—for the poets incorporated, remodelled, adapted or invented, as occasion suggested. It was also the half-formed ὕλη, the " temper of the age " (an unsatis-factory phrase), a preparedness, a habit on the part of the public, to respond to particular stimuli. There is a book to be written on the commonplaces of any great dramatic period, the handling of Fate or Death, the recurrence of mood, tone, situation. We should see then just how *little* each poet had to do ; only so much as would make a play his, only what was really essential to make it different from anyone else's. When there is this economy of effort it is possible to have several, even many, good poets at once. The great ages did not perhaps *produce* much more talent than ours ; but less talent was wasted.

Now in a formless age there is very little hope for the minor poet to do anything worth doing ; and when I say minor I mean very good poets indeed : such as filled the Greek anthology and the Eliza-bethan song-books ; even a Herrick ; but not merely second-rate poets, for Denham and Waller have quite another importance, occupying points in the development of a major form. When everything is set out for the minor poet to do, he may quite fre-quently come upon some *trouvaille*, even in the drama : Peele and Brome are examples. Under the present conditions, the minor poet has too much to do. And this leads to another reason for the incom-petence of our time in poetic drama.

Permanent literature is always a presentation : either a presentation of thought, or a presentation

of feeling by a statement of events in human action
or objects in the external world. In earlier literature—to avoid the word " classic "—we find both
kinds, and sometimes, as in some of the dialogues of
Plato, exquisite combinations of both. Aristotle
presents thought, stripped to the essential structure,
and he is a great *writer*. The *Agamemnon* or *Macbeth* is equally a statement, but of events. They
are as much works of the " intellect " as the writings
of Aristotle. There are more recent works of art
which have the same quality of intellect in common
with those of Æschylus and Shakespeare and Aristotle : *Education Sentimentale* is one of them. Compare it with such a book as *Vanity Fair* and you will
see that the labour of the intellect consisted largely
in a purification, in keeping out a great deal that
Thackeray allowed to remain in ; in refraining from
reflection, in putting into the statement enough to
make reflection unnecessary. The case of Plato is
still more illuminating. Take the *Theætetus*. In a
few opening words Plato gives a scene, a personality,
a feeling, which colour the subsequent discourse but
do not interfere with it : the particular setting, and
the abstruse theory of knowledge afterwards developed, co-operate without confusion. Could any
contemporary author exhibit such control ?

In the nineteenth century another mentality mani-
fested itself. It is evident in a very able and brilliant poem, Goethe's *Faust*. Marlowe's Mephisto-
pheles is a simpler creature than Goethe's. But at
least Marlowe has, in a few words, concentrated him

into a statement. He is there, and (incidentally) he renders Milton's Satan superfluous. Goethe's demon inevitably sends us back to Goethe. He embodies a philosophy. A creation of art should not do that : he should *replace* the philosophy. Goethe has not, that is to say, sacrificed or consecrated his thought to make the drama ; the drama is still a means. And this type of mixed art has been repeated by men incomparably smaller than Goethe. We have had one other remarkable work of this type : *Peer Gynt*. And we have had the plays of M. Maeterlinck and M. Claudel.[1]

In the works of Maeterlinck and Claudel on the one hand, and those of M. Bergson on the other, we have the mixture of the genres in which our age delights. Every work of imagination must have a philosophy ; and every philosophy must be a work of art—how often have we heard that M. Bergson is an artist ! It is a boast of his disciples. It is what the word " art " means to them that is the disputable point. Certain works of philosophy can be called works of art : much of Aristotle and Plato, Spinoza, parts of Hume, Mr. Bradley's *Principles of Logic*, Mr. Russell's essay on " Denoting " : clear and beautifully formed thought. But this is not what the admirers of Bergson, Claudel, or Maeter-

[1] I should except *The Dynasts*. This gigantic panorama is hardly to be called a success, but it is essentially an attempt to present a vision, and " sacrifices " the philosophy to the vision, as all great dramas do. Mr. Hardy has apprehended his matter as a poet and an artist.

linck (the philosophy of the latter is a little out of date) mean. They mean precisely what is not clear, but what is an emotional stimulus. And as a mixture of thought and of vision provides more stimulus, by suggesting both, both clear thinking and clear statement of particular objects must disappear.

The undigested " idea " or philosophy, the idea-emotion, is to be found also in poetic dramas which are conscientious attempts to adapt a true structure, Athenian or Elizabethan, to contemporary feeling. It appears sometimes as the attempt to supply the defect of structure by an internal structure. " But most important of all is the structure of the incidents. For Tragedy is an imitation, not of men, but of an action and of life, and life consists in action, and its end is a mode of action, not a quality." [1]

We have on the one hand the " poetic " drama, imitation Greek, imitation Elizabethan, or modern-philosophical, on the other the comedy of " ideas," from Shaw to Galsworthy, down to the ordinary social comedy. The most ramshackle Guitry farce has some paltry idea or comment upon life put into the mouth of one of the characters at the end. It is said that the stage can be used for a variety of purposes, that in only one of them perhaps is it united with literary art. A mute theatre is a possibility (I do not mean the cinema) ; the ballet is an actuality (though under-nourished) ; opera is an institution ; but where you have " imitations of life "

[1] *Poetics*, vi. 9. Butcher's translation.

on the stage, with speech, the only standard that we can allow is the standard of the work of art, aiming at the same intensity at which poetry and the other forms of art aim. From that point of view the Shavian drama is a hybrid as the Maeterlinckian drama is, and we need express no surprise at their belonging to the same epoch. Both philosophies are popularizations : the moment an idea has been transferred from its pure state in order that it may become comprehensible to the inferior intelligence it has lost contact with art. It can remain pure only by being stated simply in the form of general truth, or by being transmuted, as the attitude of Flaubert toward the small bourgeois is transformed in *Education Sentimentale*. It has there become so identified with the reality that you can no longer say what the idea is.

The essential is not, of course, that drama should be written in verse, or that we should be able to extenuate our appreciation of broad farce by occasionally attending a performance of a play of Euripides where Professor Murray's translation is sold at the door. The essential is to get upon the stage this precise statement of life which is at the same time a point of view, a world—a world which the author's mind has subjected to a complete process of simplification. I do not find that any drama which " embodies a philosophy " of the author's (like *Faust*) or which illustrates any social theory (like Shaw's) can possibly fulfil the requirements—though a place might be left for Shaw if not for Goethe.

And the world of Ibsen and the world of Tchehov are not enough simplified, universal.

Finally, we must take into account the instability of any art—the drama, music, dancing—which depends upon representation by performers. The intervention of performers introduces a complication of economic conditions which is in itself likely to be injurious. A struggle, more or less unconscious, between the creator and the interpreter is almost inevitable. The interest of a performer is almost certain to be centred in himself: a very slight acquaintance with actors and musicians will testify. The performer is interested not in form but in opportunities for virtuosity or in the communication of his " personality "; the formlessness, the lack of intellectual clarity and distinction in modern music, the great physical stamina and physical training which it often requires, are perhaps signs of the triumph of the performer. The consummation of the triumph of the actor over the play is perhaps the productions of the Guitry.

The conflict is one which certainly cannot be terminated by the utter rout of the actor profession. For one thing, the stage appeals to too many demands besides the demand for art for that to be possible ; and also we need, unfortunately, something more than refined automatons. Occasionally attempts have been made to " get around " the actor, to envelop him in masks, to set up a few " conventions " for him to stumble over, or even to develop little breeds of actors for some special Art

drama. This meddling with nature seldom succeeds ; nature usually overcomes these obstacles.
Possibly the majority of attempts to confect a poetic
drama have begun at the wrong end ; they have
aimed at the small public which wants " poetry."
(" Novices," says Aristotle, " in the art attain to
finish of diction and precision of portraiture before
they can construct the plot.") The Elizabethan
drama was aimed at a public which wanted *entertainment* of a crude sort, but would *stand* a good deal of
poetry ; our problem should be to take a form of
entertainment, and subject it to the process which
would leave it a form of art. Perhaps the music-
hall comedian is the best material. I am aware
that this is a dangerous suggestion to make. For
every person who is likely to consider it seriously
there are a dozen toymakers who would leap to
tickle æsthetic society into one more quiver and
giggle of art debauch. Very few treat art seriously.
There are those who treat it solemnly, and will continue to write poetic pastiches of Euripides and
Shakespeare ; and there are others who treat it as a
joke.

EURIPIDES AND PROFESSOR MURRAY

THE recent appearance of Miss Sybil Thorndyke as Medea at the Holborn Empire is
an event which has a bearing upon three
subjects of considerable interest : the drama, the
present standing of Greek literature, and the importance of good contemporary translation. On the
occasion on which I was present the performance was
certainly a success ; the audience was large, it was
attentive, and its applause was long. Whether the
success was due to Euripides is uncertain ; whether
it was due to Professor Murray is not proved ; but
that it was in considerable measure due to Miss
Thorndyke there is no doubt. To have held the
centre of the stage for two hours in a rôle which
requires both extreme violence and restraint, a rôle
which requires simple force and subtle variation ; to
have sustained so difficult a rôle almost without sup-
port ; this was a legitimate success. The audience, or
what could be seen of it from one of the cheaper
seats, was serious and respectful and perhaps inclined to self-approval at having attended the performance of a Greek play ; but Miss Thorndyke's
acting might have held almost any audience. It

employed all the conventions, the theatricalities, of the modern stage ; yet her personality triumphed over not only Professor Murray's verse but her own training.

The question remains whether the production was a " work of art." The rest of the cast appeared slightly ill at ease ; the nurse was quite a tolerable nurse of the crone type ; Jason was negative ; the messenger was uncomfortable at having to make such a long speech ; and the refined Dalcroze chorus had mellifluous voices which rendered their lyrics happily inaudible. All this contributed toward the high-brow effect which is so depressing ; and we imagine that the actors of Athens, who had to speak clearly enough for 20,000 auditors to be able to criticize the versification, would have been pelted with figs and olives had they mumbled so unintelligibly as most of this troupe. But the Greek actor spoke in his own language, and our actors were forced to speak in the language of Professor Gilbert Murray. So that on the whole we may say that the performance was an interesting one.

I do not believe, however, that such performances will do very much to rehabilitate Greek literature or our own, unless they stimulate a desire for better translations. The serious auditors, many of whom I observed to be like myself provided with Professor Murray's eighteenpenny translation, were probably not aware that Miss Thorndyke, in order to succeed as well as she did, was really engaged in a struggle against the translator's verse. She triumphed over it by attracting our attention to her expression and tone and making us neglect her words ; and this, of course, was not the dramatic method of Greek acting at its best. The English and Greek languages remained where they were. But few persons realize that the Greek language and the Latin language, and, *therefore*, we say, the English language, are within our lifetime passing through a critical period. The Classics have, during the latter part of the nineteenth century and up to the present moment, lost their place as a pillar of the social and political system—such as the Established Church still is. If they are to survive, to justify themselves as literature, as an element in the European mind, as the foundation for the literature we hope to create, they are very badly in need of persons capable of expounding them. We need some one—not a member of the Church of Rome, and perhaps preferably not a member of the Church of England—to explain how vital a matter it is, if Aristotle may be said to have been a moral pilot of Europe, whether we shall or shall not drop that pilot. And we need a number of educated poets who shall at least have opinions about Greek drama, and whether it is or is not of any use to us. And it must be said that Professor Gilbert Murray is not the man for this. Greek poetry will never have the slightest vitalizing effect upon English poetry if it can only appear masquerading as a vulgar debasement of the eminently personal idiom of Swinburne. These are strong words to use against the most popular Hellenist of his time ; but we must

witness of Professor Murray ere we die that these
things are not otherwise but thus.

This is really a point of capital importance. That
the most conspicuous Greek propagandist of the
day should almost habitually use two words where
the Greek language requires one, and where the
English language will provide him with one ; that
he should render σκιάν by " *grey* shadow " ; and
that he should stretch the Greek brevity to fit the
loose frame of William Morris, and blur the Greek
lyric to the fluid haze of Swinburne ; these are not
faults of infinitesimal insignificance. The first great
speech of Medea Mr. Murray begins with :

> Women of Corinth, I am come to show
> My face, lest ye despise me. . . .

We find in the Greek, ἐξῆλθον δόμων. " Show my
face," therefore, is Mr. Murray's gift.

> This thing undreamed of, sudden from on high,
> Hath sapped my soul : I dazzle where I stand,
> The cup of all life shattered in my hand. . . .

Again, we find that the Greek is :

> ἐμοὶ δ' ἄελπτον πρᾶγμα προσπεσὸν τόδε
> ψυχὴν διέφθαρκ'· οἴχομαι δὲ καὶ βίου
> χάριν μεθεῖσα κατθανεῖν χρῄζω, φίλαι.

So, here are two striking phrases which we owe to
Mr. Murray ; it is he who has sapped our soul and
shattered the cup of all life for Euripides. And
these are only random examples.

οὐκ ἔστιν ἄλλη φρὴν μιαιφονωτέρα

becomes " no bloodier spirit between heaven and hell " ! Surely we know that Professor Murray is acquainted with " Sister Helen " ? Professor Murray has simply interposed between Euripides and ourselves a barrier more impenetrable than the Greek language. We do not reproach him for preferring, apparently, Euripides to Æschylus. But if he does, he should at least appreciate Euripides. And it is inconceivable that anyone with a genuine feeling for the sound of Greek verse should deliberately elect the William Morris couplet, the Swinburne lyric, as a just equivalent.

As a poet, Mr. Murray is merely a very insignificant follower of the pre-Raphaelite movement. As a Hellenist, he is very much of the present day, and a very important figure in the day. This day began, in a sense, with Tylor and a few German anthropologists ; since then we have acquired sociology and social psychology, we have watched the clinics of Ribot and Janet, we have read books from Vienna and heard a discourse of Bergson ; a philosophy arose at Cambridge ; social emancipation crawled abroad ; our historical knowledge has of course increased ; and we have a curious Freudian-social-mystical-rationalistic-higher-critical interpretation of the Classics and what used to be called the Scriptures. I do not deny the very great value of all work by scientists in their own departments, the great interest also of this work in detail and in its consequences. Few books are more fascinating

than those of Miss Harrison, Mr. Cornford, or Mr.
Cooke, when they burrow in the origins of Greek
myths and rites ; M. Durkheim, with his social consciousness, and M. Levy-Bruhl, with his Bororo
Indians who convince themselves that they are
parroquets, are delightful writers. A number of
sciences have sprung up in an almost tropical exub-
erance which undoubtedly excites our admiration,
and the garden, not unnaturally, has come to resemble a jungle. Such men as Tylor, and Robertson
Smith, and Wilhelm Wundt, who early fertilized
the soil, would hardly recognize the resulting vege-
tation ; and indeed poor Wundt's *Völkerpsychologie*
was a musty relic before it was translated.

All these events are useful and important in their
phase, and they have sensibly affected our attitude
towards the Classics ; and it is this phase of classical
study that Professor Murray—the friend and in-
spirer of Miss Jane Harrison—represents. The Greek
is no longer the awe-inspiring Belvedere of Winckel-
mann, Goethe, and Schopenhauer, the figure of
which Walter Pater and Oscar Wilde offered us a
slightly debased re-edition. And we realize better
how different—not how much more Olympian—
were the conditions of the Greek civilization from
ours ; and at the same time Mr. Zimmern has shown
us how the Greek dealt with analogous problems.
Incidentally we do not believe that a good English
prose style can be modelled upon Cicero, or Tacitus,
or Thucydides. If Pindar bores us, we admit it ;
we are not certain that Sappho was *very* much greater

than Catullus; we hold various opinions about Vergil; and we think more highly of Petronius than our grandfathers did.

It is to be hoped that we may be grateful to Professor Murray and his friends for what they have done, while we endeavour to neutralize Professor Murray's influence upon Greek literature and English language in his translations by making better translations. The choruses from Euripides by H. D. are, allowing for errors and even occasional omissions of difficult passages, much nearer to both Greek and English than Mr. Murray's. But H. D. and the other poets of the "Poets' Translation Series" have so far done no more than pick up some of the more romantic crumbs of Greek literature; none of them has yet shown himself competent to attack the *Agamemnon*. If we are to digest the heavy food of historical and scientific knowledge that we have eaten we must be prepared for much greater exertions. We need a digestion which can assimilate both Homer and Flaubert. We need a careful study of Renaissance Humanists and Translators, such as Mr. Pound has begun. We need an eye which can see the past in its place with its definite differences from the present, and yet so lively that it shall be as present to us as the present. This is the creative eye; and it is because Professor Murray has no creative instinct that he leaves Euripides quite dead.

4

" RHETORIC " AND POETIC DRAMA

THE death of Rostand is the disappearance of the poet whom, more than any other in France, we treated as the exponent of " rhetoric," thinking of rhetoric as something recently out of fashion. And as we find ourselves looking back rather tenderly upon the author of *Cyrano* we wonder what this vice or quality is that is associated as plainly with Rostand's merits as with his defects. His rhetoric, at least, suited him at times so well, and so much better than it suited a much greater poet, Baudelaire, who is at times as rhetorical as Rostand. And we begin to suspect that the word is merely a vague term of abuse for any style that is bad, that is so evidently bad or second-rate that we do not recognize the necessity for greater precision in the phrases we apply to it.

Our own Elizabethan and Jacobean poetry—in so nice a problem it is much safer to stick to one's own language—is repeatedly called " rhetorical." It had this and that notable quality, but, when we wish to admit that it had defects, it is rhetorical. It had serious defects, even gross faults, but we cannot be considered to have erased them from our language when we are so unclear in our perception of what

78

they are. The fact is that both Elizabethan prose and Elizabethan poetry are written in a variety of styles with a variety of vices. Is the style of Lyly, is Euphuism, rhetorical ? In contrast to the elder style of Ascham and Elyot which it assaults, it is a clear, flowing, orderly and relatively pure style, with a systematic if monotonous formula of antitheses and similes. Is the style of Nashe ? A tumid, flatulent, vigorous style very different from Lyly's. Or it is perhaps the strained and the mixed figures of speech in which Shakespeare indulged himself. Or it is perhaps the careful declamation of Jonson. The word simply cannot be used as synonymous with bad writing. The meanings which it has been obliged to shoulder have been mostly opprobrious ; but if a precise meaning can be found for it this meaning may occasionally represent a virtue. It is one of those words which it is the business of criticism to dissect and reassemble. Let us avoid the assumption that rhetoric is a vice of manner, and endeavour to find a rhetoric of substance also, which is right because it issues from what it has to express.

At the present time there is a manifest preference for the " conversational " in poetry—the style of " direct speech," opposed to the " oratorical " and the rhetorical ; but if rhetoric is any convention of writing inappropriately applied, this conversational style can and does become a rhetoric—or what is supposed to be a conversational style, for it is often as remote from polite discourse as well could be. Much of the second and third rate in American *vers libre* is of this sort ; and much of the second and third rate in English Wordsworthianism. There is in fact no conversational or other form which can be applied indiscriminately ; if a writer wishes to give the effect of speech he must positively give the effect of himself talking in his own person or in one of his rôles ; and if we are to express ourselves, our variety of thoughts and feelings, on a variety of subjects with inevitable rightness, we must adapt our manner to the moment with infinite variations. Examination of the development of Elizabethan drama shows this progress in adaptation, a development from monotony to variety, a progressive refinement in the perception of the variations of feeling, and a progressive elaboration of the means of expressing these variations. This drama is admitted to have grown away from the rhetorical expression, the bombast speeches, of Kyd and Marlowe to the subtle and dispersed utterance of Shakespeare and Webster. But this apparent abandonment or outgrowth of rhetoric is two things : it is partly an improvement in language and it is partly progressive variation in feeling. There is, of course, a long distance separating the furibund fluency of old Hieronimo and the broken words of Lear. There is also a difference between the famous

> Oh eyes no eyes, but fountains full of tears !
> Oh life no life, but lively form of death !

and the superb " additions to Hieronimo." [1]

[1] Of the authorship it can only be said that the lines are by some admirer of Marlowe. This might well be Jonson.

We think of Shakespeare perhaps as the dramatist who concentrates everything into a sentence, " Pray you undo this button," or " Honest honest Iago " ; we forget that there is a rhetoric proper to Shakespeare at his best period which is quite free from the genuine Shakespearean vices either of the early period or the late. These passages are comparable to the best bombast of Kyd or Marlowe, with a greater command of language and a greater control of the emotion. *The Spanish Tragedy* is bombastic when it descends to language which was only the trick of its age ; *Tamburlaine* is bombastic because it is monotonous, inflexible to the alterations of emotion. The really fine rhetoric of Shakespeare occurs in situations where a character in the play *sees himself* in a dramatic light :

Othello.   And say, besides,—that in Aleppo once . . .

Coriolanus.   If you have writ your annals true, 'tis there,
That like an eagle in a dovecote, I
Fluttered your Volscians in Corioli.
Alone I did it.   Boy !

Timon.   Come not to me again ; but say to Athens,
Timon hath made his everlasting mansion
Upon the beachèd verge of the salt flood . . .

It occurs also once in *Antony and Cleopatra*, when Enobarbus is inspired to see Cleopatra in this dramatic light :

The barge she sat in . . .

Shakespeare made fun of Marston, and Jonson made fun of Kyd. But in Marston's play the words were

expressive of nothing ; and Jonson was criticizing
the feeble and conceited language, not the emotion,
not the "oratory." Jonson is as oratorical himself,
and the moments when his oratory succeeds are, I
believe, the moments that conform to our formula.
Notably the speech of Sylla's ghost in the induction
to *Catiline*, and the speech of Envy at the beginning
of *The Poetaster*. These two figures are contemplating their own dramatic importance, and quite
properly. But in the Senate speeches in *Catiline*,
how tedious, how dusty ! Here we are spectators
not of a play of characters, but of a play of forensic,
exactly as if we had been forced to attend the sitting
itself. A speech in a play should never appear to
be intended to move us as it might conceivably
move other characters in the play, for it is essential
that we should preserve our position of spectators,
and observe always from the outside though with
complete understanding. The scene in *Julius Cæsar*
is right because the object of our attention is not the
speech of Antony (*Bedeutung*) but the effect of his
speech upon the mob, and Antony's intention, his
preparation and consciousness of the effect. And
in the rhetorical speeches from Shakespeare which
have been cited, we have this necessary advantage
of a new clue to the character, in noting the angle
from which he views himself. But when a character
in a play makes a direct appeal to us, we are either
the victims of our own sentiment, or we are in the
presence of a vicious rhetoric.

These references ought to supply some evidence

of the propriety of Cyrano on Noses. Is not Cyrano exactly in this position of contemplating himself as a romantic, a dramatic figure ? This dramatic sense on the part of the characters themselves is rare in modern drama. In sentimental drama it appears in a degraded form, when we are evidently intended to accept the character's sentimental interpretation of himself. In plays of realism we often find parts which are never allowed to be consciously dramatic, for fear, perhaps, of their appearing less real. But in actual life, in many of those situations in actual life which we enjoy consciously and keenly, we are at times aware of ourselves in this way, and these moments are of very great usefulness to dramatic verse. A very small part of acting is that which takes place on the stage ! Rostand had—whether he had anything else or not—this dramatic sense, and it is what gives life to Cyrano. It is a sense which is almost a sense of humour (for when anyone is conscious of himself as acting, something like a sense of humour is present). It gives Rostand's characters—Cyrano at least—a gusto which is uncommon on the modern stage. No doubt Rostand's people play up to this too steadily. We recognize that in the love scenes of Cyrano in the garden, for in *Romeo and Juliet* the profounder dramatist shows his lovers melting into incoherent unconsciousness of their isolated selves, shows the human soul in the process of forgetting itself. Rostand could not do that ; but in the particular case of Cyrano on Noses, the character, the situation, the occasion were perfectly suited and combined. The tirade generated by this combination is not only genuinely and highly dramatic : it is possibly poetry also. If a writer is incapable of composing such a scene as this, so much the worse for his poetic drama.

Cyrano satisfies, as far as scenes like this can satisfy, the requirements of poetic drama. It must take genuine and substantial human emotions, such emotions as observation can confirm, typical emotions, and give them artistic form ; the degree of abstraction is a question for the method of each author. In Shakespeare the form is determined in the unity of the whole, as well as single scenes ; it is something to attain this unity, as Rostand does, in scenes if not the whole play. Not only as a dramatist, but as a poet, he is superior to Maeterlinck, whose drama, in failing to be dramatic, fails also to be poetic. Maeterlinck has a literary perception of the dramatic and a literary perception of the poetic, and he joins the two ; the two are not, as sometimes they are in the work of Rostand, fused. His characters take no conscious delight in their rôle—they are sentimental. With Rostand the centre of gravity is in the expression of the emotion, not as with Maeterlinck in the emotion which cannot be expressed. Some writers appear to believe that emotions gain in intensity through being inarticulate. Perhaps the emotions are not significant enough to endure full daylight.

In any case, we may take our choice : we may apply the term " rhetoric " to the type of dramatic

speech which I have instanced, and then we must
admit that it covers good as well as bad. Or we may
choose to except this type of speech from rhetoric.
In that case we must say that rhetoric is any adorn-
ment or inflation of speech which is *not done for a
particular effect* but for a general impressiveness.
And in this case, too, we cannot allow the term to
cover all bad writing.

NOTES ON THE BLANK VERSE OF
CHRISTOPHER MARLOWE

" Marloe was stabd with a dagger, and dyed swearing "

A MORE friendly critic, Mr. A. C. Swinburne, observes of this poet that " the father of English tragedy and the creator of English blank verse was therefore also the teacher and the guide of Shakespeare." In this sentence there are two misleading assumptions and two misleading conclusions. Kyd has as good a title to the first honour as Marlowe ; Surrey has a better title to the second ; and Shakespeare was not taught or guided by one of his predecessors or contemporaries alone. The less questionable judgment is, that Marlowe exercised a strong influence over later drama, though not himself as great a dramatist as Kyd ; that he introduced several new tones into blank verse, and commenced the dissociative process which drew it farther and farther away from the rhythms of rhymed verse ; and that when Shakespeare borrowed from him, which was pretty often at the beginning, Shakespeare either made something inferior or something different.

The comparative study of English versification at various periods is a large tract of unwritten history.

To make a study of blank verse alone, would be to elicit some curious conclusions. It would show, I believe, that blank verse within Shakespeare's lifetime was more highly developed, that it became the vehicle of more varied and more intense art-emotions than it has ever conveyed since ; and that after the erection of the Chinese Wall of Milton, blank verse has suffered not only arrest but retrogression. That the blank verse of Tennyson, for example, a consummate master of this form in certain applications, is cruder (*not* " rougher " or less perfect in technique) than that of half a dozen contemporaries of Shakespeare ; cruder, because less capable of expressing complicated, subtle, and surprising emotions.

Every writer who has written any blank verse worth saving has produced particular tones which his verse and no other's is capable of rendering ; and we should keep this in mind when we talk about " influences " and " indebtedness." Shakespeare is " universal " (if you like) because he has more of these tones than anyone else ; but they are all out of the one man ; one man cannot be more than one man ; there might have been six Shakespeares at once without conflicting frontiers ; and to say that Shakespeare expressed nearly all human emotions, implying that he left very little for anyone else, is a radical misunderstanding of art and the artist—a misunderstanding which, even when explicitly rejected, may lead to our neglecting the effort of attention necessary to discover the specific properties of the verse of Shakespeare's contemporaries. The development of blank verse may be likened to the analysis of that astonishing industrial product coal-tar. Marlowe's verse is one of the earlier derivatives, but it possesses properties which are not repeated in any of the analytic or synthetic blank verses discovered somewhat later.

The " vices of style " of Marlowe's and Shakespeare's age is a convenient name for a number of vices, no one of which, perhaps, was shared by all of the writers. It is pertinent, at least, to remark that Marlowe's " rhetoric " is not, or not characteristically, Shakespeare's rhetoric ; that Marlowe's rhetoric consists in a pretty simple huffe-snuffe bombast, while Shakespeare's is more exactly a vice of style, a tortured perverse ingenuity of images which dissipates instead of concentrating the imagination, and which may be due in part to influences by which Marlowe was untouched. Next, we find that Marlowe's vice is one which he was gradually attenuating, and even, what is more miraculous, turning into a virtue. And we find that this bard of torrential imagination recognized many of his best bits (and those of one or two others), saved them, and reproduced them more than once, almost invariably improving them in the process.

It is worth while noticing a few of these versions, because they indicate, somewhat contrary to usual opinion, that Marlowe was a deliberate and conscious workman. Mr. J. M. Robertson has spotted an interesting theft of Marlowe's from Spenser. Here is Spenser (*Faery Queen*, I. vii. 32) :

> Like to an almond tree y-mounted high
>   On top of green Selinis all alone,
> With blossoms brave bedeckèd daintily;
>   Whose tender locks do tremble every one
> At every little breath that under heaven is blown.

And here Marlowe (*Tamburlaine*, Part II. Act iv. sc. iii.):

> Like to an almond tree y-mounted high
> Upon the lofty and celestial mount
> Of evergreen Selinus, quaintly deck'd
> With blooms more white than Erycina's brows,
> Whose tender blossoms tremble every one
> At every little breath that thorough heaven is blown.

This is interesting, not only as showing that Marlowe's talent, like that of most poets, was partly synthetic, but also because it seems to give a clue to some particularly " lyric " effects found in *Tamburlaine*, not in Marlowe's other plays, and not, I believe, anywhere else. For example, the praise of Zenocrate in Part II. Act II. sc. iv.:

> Now walk the angels on the walls of heaven,
> As sentinels to warn th' immortal souls
> To entertain divine Zenocrate: etc.

This is not Spenser's movement, but the influence of Spenser must be present. There had been no great blank verse before Marlowe; but there was the powerful presence of this great master of melody immediately precedent; and the combination produced results which could not be repeated. I do not think that it can be claimed that Peele had any influence here.

The passage quoted from Spenser has a further interest. It will be noted that the fourth line :

With blooms more white than Erycina's brows

is Marlowe's contribution. Compare this with these other lines of Marlowe :

> So looks my love, shadowing in her brows
> (*Tamburlaine*)
>
> Like to the shadows of Pyramides
> (*Tamburlaine*)

and the final and best version :

> Shadowing more beauty in their airy brows
> Then have the white breasts of the queen of love
> (*Doctor Faustus*)

and compare the whole set with Spenser again (*F. Q.*) :

> Upon her eyelids many graces sate
> Under the shadow of her even brows,

a passage which Mr. Robertson says Spenser himself used in three other places.

This economy is frequent in Marlowe. Within *Tamburlaine* it occurs in the form of monotony, especially in the facile use of resonant names (*e.g.* the recurrence of " Caspia " or " Caspian " with the same tone effect), a practice in which Marlowe was followed by Milton, but which Marlowe himself outgrew. Again,

> Zenocrate, lovlier than the love of Jove,
> Brighter than is the silver Rhodope,

is paralleled later by

> Zenocrate, the lovliest maid alive,
> Fairier than rocks of pearl and precious stone.

One line Marlowe remodels with triumphant success :

> And set black streamers in the firmament
> (*Tamburlaine*)

becomes

> See, see, where Christ's blood streams in the firmament !
> (*Doctor Faustus*)

The verse accomplishments of *Tamburlaine* are notably two : Marlowe gets into blank verse the melody of Spenser, and he gets a new driving power by reinforcing the sentence period against the line period. The rapid long sentence, running line into line, as in the famous soliloquies " Nature compounded of four elements " and " What is beauty, saith my sufferings, then ? " marks the certain escape of blank verse from the rhymed couplet, and from the elegiac or rather pastoral note of Surrey, to which Tennyson returned. If you contrast these two soliloquies with the verse of Marlowe's greatest contemporary, Kyd—by no means a despicable versifier—you see the importance of the innovation :

> The one took sanctuary, and, being sent for out,
> Was murdered in Southwark as he passed
> To Greenwich, where the Lord Protector lay.
> Black Will was burned in Flushing on a stage :
> Green was hanged at Osbridge in Kent . . .

which is not really inferior to :

> So these four abode
> Within one house together ; and as years
> Went forward, Mary took another mate ;
> But Dora lived unmarried till her death.
>
> (Tennyson, *Dora*)

In *Faustus* Marlowe went farther : he broke up the line, to a gain in intensity, in the last soliloquy ; and he developed a new and important conversational tone in the dialogues of Faustus with the devil. *Edward II.* has never lacked consideration : it is more desirable, in brief space, to remark upon two plays, one of which has been misunderstood and the other underrated. These are the *Jew of Malta* and *Dido Queen of Carthage*. Of the first of these, it has always been said that the end, even the last two acts, are unworthy of the first three. If one takes the *Jew of Malta* not as a tragedy, or as a " tragedy of blood," but as a farce, the concluding act becomes intelligible ; and if we attend with a careful ear to the versification, we find that Marlowe develops a tone to suit this farce, and even perhaps that this tone is his most powerful and mature tone. I say farce, but with the enfeebled humour of our times the word is a misnomer ; it is the farce of the old English humour, the terribly serious, even savage comic humour, the humour which spent its last breath on the decadent genius of Dickens. It has nothing in common with J. M. Barrie, Captain Bairnsfather, or *Punch*. It is the humour of that very serious (but very different) play, *Volpone*.

> First, be thou void of these affections,
> Compassion, love, vain hope, and heartless fear ;
> Be moved at nothing, see thou pity none . . .
> As for myself, I walk abroad o' nights,
> And kill sick people groaning under walls :
> Sometimes I go about and poison wells . . .

and the last words of Barabas complete this prodigious caricature :

> But now begins th' extremity of heat
> To pinch me with intolerable pangs :
> Die, life ! fly, soul ! tongue, curse thy fill, and die !

It is something which Shakespeare could not do, and which he could not have understood.

Dido appears to be a hurried play, perhaps done to order with the *Æneid* in front of him. But even here there is progress. The account of the sack of Troy is in this newer style of Marlowe's, this style which secures its emphasis by always hesitating on the edge of caricature at the right moment :

The Grecian soldiers, tir'd with ten years war,
Began to cry, " Let us unto our ships,
Troy is invincible, why stay we here ? " . . .

By this, the camp was come unto the walls,
And through the breach did march into the streets,
Where, meeting with the rest, " Kill, kill ! " they cried. . . .

And after him, his band of Myrmidons,
With balls of wild-fire in their murdering paws . . .

At last, the soldiers pull'd her by the heels,
And swung her howling in the empty air. . . .

We saw Cassandra sprawling in the streets . . .

This is not Vergil, or Shakespeare ; it is pure
Marlowe. By comparing the whole speech with
Clarence's dream, in *Richard III.*, one acquires a
little insight into the difference between Marlowe
and Shakespeare :

> What scourge for perjury
> Can this dark monarchy afford false Clarence ?

There, on the other hand, is what Marlowe's
style could not do ; the phrase has a concision
which is almost classical, certainly Dantesque.
Again, as often with the Elizabethan dramatists,
there are lines in Marlowe, besides the many lines
that Shakespeare adapted, that might have been
written by either :

> If thou wilt stay,
> Leap in mine arms ; mine arms are open wide ;
> If not, turn from me, and I'll turn from thee ;
> For though thou hast the heart to say farewell,
> I have not power to stay thee.

But the direction in which Marlowe's verse might
have moved, had he not " dyed swearing," is quite
un-Shakespearean, is toward this intense and
serious and indubitably great poetry, which, like
some great painting and sculpture, attains its
effects by something not unlike caricature.

HAMLET AND HIS PROBLEMS

FEW critics have even admitted that *Hamlet* the play is the primary problem, and Hamlet the character only secondary. And Hamlet the character has had an especial temptation for that most dangerous type of critic : the critic with a mind which is naturally of the creative order, but which through some weakness in creative power exercises itself in criticism instead. These minds often find in Hamlet a vicarious existence for their own artistic realization. Such a mind had Goethe, who made of Hamlet a Werther ; and such had Coleridge, who made of Hamlet a Coleridge ; and probably neither of these men in writing about Hamlet remembered that his first business was to study a work of art. The kind of criticism that Goethe and Coleridge produced, in writing of Hamlet, is the most misleading kind possible. For they both possessed unquestionable critical insight, and both make their critical aberrations the more plausible by the substitution—of their own Hamlet for Shakespeare's—which their creative gift effects. We should be thankful that Walter Pater did not fix his attention on this play.

Two recent writers, Mr. J. M. Robertson and

Professor Stoll of the University of Minnesota, have
issued small books which can be praised for moving
in the other direction. Mr. Stoll performs a service in recalling to our attention the labours of the
critics of the seventeenth and eighteenth centuries,[1]
observing that

they knew less about psychology than more recent
Hamlet critics, but they were nearer in spirit to Shakespeare's art ; and as they insisted on the importance of
the effect of the whole rather than on the importance
of the leading character, they were nearer, in their old-
fashioned way, to the secret of dramatic art in general.

Qua work of art, the work of art cannot be inter-
preted ; there is nothing to interpret ; we can only
criticize it according to standards, in comparison to
other works of art ; and for " interpretation " the
chief task is the presentation of relevant historical
facts which the reader is not assumed to know.
Mr. Robertson points out, very pertinently, how
critics have failed in their " interpretation " of *Hamlet* by ignoring what ought to be very obvious : that
Hamlet is a stratification, that it represents the efforts
of a series of men, each making what he could out
of the work of his predecessors. The *Hamlet* of
Shakespeare will appear to us very differently if,
instead of treating the whole action of the play as
due to Shakespeare's design, we perceive his *Hamlet*

[1] I have never, by the way, seen a cogent refutation of
Thomas Rymer's objections to *Othello.*

to be superposed upon much cruder material which persists even in the final form.

We know that there was an older play by Thomas Kyd, that extraordinary dramatic (if not poetic) genius who was in all probability the author of two plays so dissimilar as the *Spanish Tragedy* and *Arden of Feversham* ; and what this play was like we can guess from three clues : from the *Spanish Tragedy* itself, from the tale of Belleforest upon which Kyd's *Hamlet* must have been based, and from a version acted in Germany in Shakespeare's lifetime which bears strong evidence of having been adapted from the earlier, not from the later, play. From these three sources it is clear that in the earlier play the motive was a revenge-motive simply ; that the action or delay is caused, as in the *Spanish Tragedy*, solely by the difficulty of assassinating a monarch surrounded by guards ; and that the " madness " of Hamlet was feigned in order to escape suspicion, and successfully. In the final play of Shakespeare, on the other hand, there is a motive which is more important than that of revenge, and which explicitly " blunts " the latter ; the delay in revenge is unexplained on grounds of necessity or expediency ; and the effect of the " madness " is not to lull but to arouse the king's suspicion. The alteration is not complete enough, however, to be convincing. Furthermore, there are verbal parallels so close to the *Spanish Tragedy* as to leave no doubt that in places Shakespeare was merely *revising* the text of Kyd. And finally there are unexplained scenes—the Polonius-Laertes and the Polonius-Reynaldo scenes—for which there is little excuse; these scenes are not in the verse style of Kyd, and not beyond doubt in the style of Shakespeare. These Mr. Robertson believes to be scenes in the original play of Kyd reworked by a third hand, perhaps Chapman, before Shakespeare touched the play. And he concludes, with very strong show of reason, that the original play of Kyd was, like certain other revenge plays, in two parts of five acts each. The upshot of Mr. Robertson's examination is, we believe, irrefragable: that Shakespeare's *Hamlet*, so far as it is Shakespeare's, is a play dealing with the effect of a mother's guilt upon her son, and that Shakespeare was unable to impose this motive successfully upon the "intractable" material of the old play.

Of the intractability there can be no doubt. So far from being Shakespeare's masterpiece, the play is most certainly an artistic failure. In several ways the play is puzzling, and disquieting as is none of the others. Of all the plays it is the longest and is possibly the one on which Shakespeare spent most pains; and yet he has left in it superfluous and inconsistent scenes which even hasty revision should have noticed. The versification is variable. Lines like

> Look, the morn, in russet mantle clad,
> Walks o'er the dew of yon high eastern hill,

are of the Shakespeare of *Romeo and Juliet*. The lines in Act v. sc. ii.,

> Sir, in my heart there was a kind of fighting
> That would not let me sleep . . .
> Up from my cabin,
> My sea-gown scarf'd about me, in the dark
> Grop'd I to find out them : had my desire ;
> Finger'd their packet ;

are of his quite mature. Both workmanship and thought are in an unstable condition. We are surely justified in attributing the play, with that other profoundly interesting play of " intractable " material and astonishing versification, *Measure for Measure*, to a period of crisis, after which follow the tragic successes which culminate in *Coriolanus*. *Coriolanus* may be not as " interesting " as *Hamlet*, but it is, with *Antony and Cleopatra*, Shakespeare's most assured artistic success. And probably more people have thought *Hamlet* a work of art because they found it interesting, than have found it interesting because it is a work of art. It is the " Mona Lisa " of literature.

The grounds of *Hamlet's* failure are not immediately obvious. Mr. Robertson is undoubtedly correct in concluding that the essential emotion of the play is the feeling of a son towards a guilty mother :

> [Hamlet's] tone is that of one who has suffered tortures on the score of his mother's degradation. . . . The guilt of a mother is an almost intolerable motive for drama, but it had to be maintained and emphasized to supply a psychological solution, or rather a hint of one.

This, however, is by no means the whole story.

It is not merely the " guilt of a mother" that cannot be handled as Shakespeare handled the suspicion of Othello, the infatuation of Antony, or the pride of Coriolanus. The subject might conceivably have expanded into a tragedy like these, intelligible, self-complete, in the sunlight. *Hamlet*, like the sonnets, is full of some stuff that the writer could not drag to light, contemplate, or manipulate into art. And when we search for this feeling, we find it, as in the sonnets, very difficult to localize. You cannot point to it in the speeches ; indeed, if you examine the two famous soliloquies you see the versification of Shakespeare, but a content which might be claimed by another, perhaps by the author of the *Revenge of Bussy d'Ambois*, Act v. sc. i. We find Shakespeare's *Hamlet* not in the action, not in any quotations that we might select, so much as in an unmistakable tone which is unmistakably not in the earlier play.

The only way of expressing emotion in the form of art is by finding an " objective correlative " ; in other words, a set of objects, a situation, a chain of events which shall be the formula of that *particular* emotion ; such that when the external facts, which must terminate in sensory experience, are given, the emotion is immediately evoked. If you examine any of Shakespeare's more successful tragedies, you will find this exact equivalence ; you will find that the state of mind of Lady Macbeth walking in her sleep has been communicated to you by a skilful accumulation of imagined sensory impressions ;

the words of Macbeth on hearing of his wife's death strike us as if, given the sequence of events, these words were automatically released by the last event in the series. The artistic " inevitability " lies in this complete adequacy of the external to the emotion ; and this is precisely what is deficient in *Hamlet*. Hamlet (the man) is dominated by an emotion which is inexpressible, because it is in *excess* of the facts as they appear. And the supposed identity of Hamlet with his author is genuine to this point : that Hamlet's bafflement at the absence of objective equivalent to his feelings is a prolongation of the bafflement of his creator in the face of his artistic problem. Hamlet is up against the difficulty that his disgust is occasioned by his mother, but that his mother is not an adequate equivalent for it ; his disgust envelops and exceeds her. It is thus a feeling which he cannot understand ; he cannot objectify it, and it therefore remains to poison life and obstruct action. None of the possible actions can satisfy it ; and nothing that Shakespeare can do with the plot can express Hamlet for him. And it must be noticed that the very nature of the *données* of the problem precludes objective equivalence. To have heightened the criminality of Gertrude would have been to provide the formula for a totally different emotion in Hamlet ; it is just *because* her character is so negative and insignificant that she arouses in Hamlet the feeling which she is incapable of representing.

The " madness " of Hamlet lay to Shakespeare's

hand ; in the earlier play a simple ruse, and to the end, we may presume, understood as a ruse by the audience. For Shakespeare it is less than madness and more than feigned. The levity of Hamlet, his repetition of phrase, his puns, are not part of a deliberate plan of dissimulation, but a form of emotional relief. In the character Hamlet it is the buffoonery of an emotion which can find no outlet in action ; in the dramatist it is the buffoonery of an emotion which he cannot express in art. The intense feeling, ecstatic or terrible, without an object or exceeding its object, is something which every person of sensibility has known ; it is doubtless a study to pathologists. It often occurs in adolescence : the ordinary person puts these feelings to sleep, or trims down his feeling to fit the business world ; the artist keeps it alive by his ability to intensify the world to his emotions. The Hamlet of Laforgue is an adolescent ; the Hamlet of Shakespeare is not, he has not that explanation and excuse. We must simply admit that here Shakespeare tackled a problem which proved too much for him. Why he attempted it at all is an insoluble puzzle ; under compulsion of what experience he attempted to express the inexpressibly horrible, we cannot ever know. We need a great many facts in his biography ; and we should like to know whether, and when, and after or at the same time as what personal experience, he read Montaigne, II. xii., *Apologie de Raimond Sebond*. We should have, finally, to know something which is by hypothesis unknowable, for we assume it to be an experience which, in the manner indicated, exceeded the facts. We should have to understand things which Shakespeare did not understand himself.

BEN JONSON

THE reputation of Jonson has been of the most deadly kind that can be compelled upon the memory of a great poet. To be universally accepted ; to be damned by the praise that quenches all desire to read the book ; to be afflicted by the imputation of the virtues which excite the least pleasure ; and to be read only by historians and antiquaries—this is the most perfect conspiracy of approval. For some generations the reputation of Jonson has been carried rather as a liability than as an asset in the balance-sheet of English literature. No critic has succeeded in making him appear pleasurable or even interesting. Swinburne's book on Jonson satisfies no curiosity and stimulates no thought. For the critical study in the " Men of Letters Series " by Mr. Gregory Smith there is a place ; it satisfies curiosity, it supplies many just observations, it provides valuable matter on the neglected masques ; it only fails to remodel the image of Jonson which is settled in our minds. Probably the fault lies with several generations of our poets. It is not that the value of poetry is only its value to living poets for their own work ; but appreciation is akin to creation, and true enjoyment of poetry is related to the stirring of suggestion, the stimulus that a poet feels in his enjoyment of other poetry. Jonson has provided no creative stimulus for a very long time ; consequently we must look back as far as Dryden—precisely, a poetic practitioner who learned from Jonson— before we find a living criticism of Jonson's work.

Yet there are possibilities for Jonson even now. We have no difficulty in seeing what brought him to this pass ; how, in contrast, not with Shakespeare, but with Marlowe, Webster, Donne, Beaumont, and Fletcher, he has been paid out with reputation instead of enjoyment. He is no less a poet than these men, but his poetry is of the surface. Poetry of the surface cannot be understood without study ; for to deal with the surface of life, as Jonson dealt with it, is to deal so deliberately that we too must be deliberate, in order to understand. Shakespeare, and smaller men also, are in the end more difficult, but they offer something at the start to encourage the student or to satisfy those who want nothing more ; they are suggestive, evocative, a phrase, a voice ; they offer poetry in detail as well as in design. So does Dante offer something, a phrase everywhere (*tu se' ombra ed ombra vedi*) even to readers who have no Italian ; and Dante and Shakespeare have poetry of design as well as of detail. But the polished veneer of Jonson reflects only the lazy reader's fatuity ; unconscious does not respond to unconscious ; no swarms of inarticulate feelings

are aroused. The immediate appeal of Jonson is
to the mind ; his emotional tone is not in the single
verse, but in the design of the whole. But not
many people are capable of discovering for themselves the beauty which is only found after labour ;
and Jonson's industrious readers have been those
whose interest was historical and curious, and those
who have thought that in discovering the historical
and curious interest they had discovered the
artistic value as well. When we say that Jonson
requires study, we do not mean study of his classical
scholarship or of seventeenth-century manners. We
mean intelligent saturation in his work as a whole ;
we mean that in order to enjoy him at all, we must
get to the centre of his work and his temperament,
and that we must see him unbiased by time, as a
contemporary. And to see him as a contemporary
does not so much require the power of putting ourselves into seventeenth-century London as it requires the power of setting Jonson in our London :
a more difficult triumph of divination.

It is generally conceded that Jonson failed as a
tragic dramatist ; and it is usually agreed that he
failed because his genius was for satiric comedy and
because of the weight of pedantic learning with
which he burdened his two tragic failures. The
second point marks an obvious error of detail ;
the first is too crude a statement to be accepted ;
to say that he failed because his genius was un-
suited to tragedy is to tell us nothing at all. Jonson
did not write a good tragedy, but we can see no

reason why he should not have written one. If two plays so different as *The Tempest* and *The Silent Woman* are both comedies, surely the category of tragedy could be made wide enough to include something possible for Jonson to have done. But the classification of tragedy and comedy, while it may be sufficient to mark the distinction in a dramatic literature of more rigid form and treatment—it may distinguish Aristophanes from Euripides—is not adequate to a drama of such variations as the Elizabethans. Tragedy is a crude classification for plays so different in their tone as *Macbeth, The Jew of Malta,* and *The Witch of Edmonton*; and it does not help us much to say that *The Merchant of Venice* and *The Alchemist* are comedies. Jonson had his own scale, his own instrument. The merit which *Catiline* possesses is the same merit that is exhibited more triumphantly in *Volpone*; *Catiline* fails, not because it is too laboured and conscious, but because it is not conscious enough; because Jonson in this play was not alert to his own idiom, not clear in his mind as to what his temperament wanted him to do. In *Catiline* Jonson conforms, or attempts to conform, to conventions; not to the conventions of antiquity, which he had exquisitely under control, but to the conventions of tragico-historical drama of his time. It is not the Latin erudition that sinks *Catiline*, but the application of that erudition to a form which was not the proper vehicle for the mind which had amassed the erudition.

If you look at *Catiline*—that dreary Pyrrhic victory of tragedy—you find two passages to be successful : Act ii. scene 1, the dialogue of the political ladies, and the Prologue of Sylla's ghost. These two passages are genial. The soliloquy of the ghost is a characteristic Jonson success in content and in versification—

Dost thou not feel me, Rome ? not yet ! is night
So heavy on thee, and my weight so light ?
Can Sylla's ghost arise within thy walls,
Less threatening than an earthquake, the quick falls
Of thee and thine ?   Shake not the frighted heads
Of thy steep towers, or shrink to their first beds ?
Or as their ruin the large Tyber fills,
Make that swell up, and drown thy seven proud hills ? . . .

This is the learned, but also the creative, Jonson. Without concerning himself with the character of Sulla, and in lines of invective, Jonson makes Sylla's ghost, while the words are spoken, a living and terrible force. The words fall with as determined beat as if they were the will of the morose Dictator himself.   You may say : merely invective ; but mere invective, even if as superior to the clumsy fisticuffs of Marston and Hall as Jonson's verse is superior to theirs, would not create a living figure as Jonson has done in this long tirade. And you may say ; rhetoric ; but if we are to call it " rhetoric " we must subject that term to a closer dissection than any to which it is accustomed. What Jonson has done here is not merely a fine speech. It is the careful, precise filling in of a strong and simple outline, and at no point does it overflow the outline ; it is far more careful and precise in its obedience to this outline than are many of the speeches in *Tamburlaine*. The outline is not Sulla, for Sulla has nothing to do with it, but " Sylla's ghost." The words may not be suitable to an historical Sulla, or to anybody in history, but they are a perfect expression for " Sylla's ghost." You cannot say they are rhetorical " because people do not talk like that," you cannot call them " verbiage " ; they do not exhibit prolixity or redundancy or the other vices in the rhetoric books ; there is a definite artistic emotion which demands expression at that length. The words themselves are mostly simple words, the syntax is natural, the language austere rather than adorned. Turning then to the induction of *The Poetaster*, we find another success of the same kind—

Light, I salute thee, but with wounded nerves . . .

Men may not talk in that way, but the spirit of envy does, and in the words of Jonson envy is a real and living person. It is not human life that informs envy and Sylla's ghost, but it is energy of which human life is only another variety.

Returning to *Catiline*, we find that the best scene in the body of the play is one which cannot be squeezed into a tragic frame, and which appears to belong to satiric comedy. The scene between Fulvia and Galla and Sempronia is a living scene in a wilderness of oratory. And as it recalls other

5

scenes—there is a suggestion of the college of ladies
in *The Silent Woman*—it looks like a comedy scene.
And it appears to be satire.

They shall all give and pay well, that come here,
If they will have it; and that, jewels, pearl,
Plate, or round sums to buy these. I'm not taken
With a cob-swan or a high-mounting bull,
As foolish Leda and Europa were;
But the bright gold, with Danaë. For such price
I would endure a rough, harsh Jupiter,
Or ten such thundering gamesters, and refrain
To laugh at 'em, till they are gone, with my much suffering.

This scene is no more comedy than it is tragedy, and
the " satire " is merely a medium for the essential
emotion. Jonson's drama is only incidentally
satire, because it is only incidentally a criticism
upon the actual world. It is not satire in the way
in which the work of Swift or the work of Molière
may be called satire : that is, it does not find its
source in any precise emotional attitude or precise
intellectual criticism of the actual world. It is
satire perhaps as the work of Rabelais is satire ;
certainly not more so. The important thing is
that if fiction can be divided into creative fiction
and critical fiction, Jonson's is creative. That he
was a great critic, our first great critic, does not
affect this assertion. Every creator is also a
critic ; Jonson was a conscious critic, but he was
also conscious in his creations. Certainly, one
sense in which the term " critical " may be applied
to fiction is a sense in which the term might be

used of a method antithetical to Jonson's. It is
the method of *Education Sentimentale*. The characters of Jonson, of Shakespeare, perhaps of all the
greatest drama, are drawn in positive and simple
outlines. They may be filled in, and by Shakespeare they are filled in, by much detail or many
shifting aspects ; but a clear and sharp and simple
form remains through these—though it would be
hard to say in what the clarity and sharpness and
simplicity of Hamlet consists. But Frédéric Moreau
is not made in that way. He is constructed partly
by negative definition, built up by a great number
of observations. We cannot isolate him from the
environment in which we find him ; it may be an
environment which is or can be much universalized ;
nevertheless it, and the figure in it, consist of very
many observed particular facts, the actual world.
Without this world the figure dissolves. The ruling
faculty is a critical perception, a commentary upon
experienced feeling and sensation. If this is true
of Flaubert, it is true in a higher degree of Molière
than of Jonson. The broad farcical lines of Molière
may seem to be the same drawing as Jonson's.
But Molière—say in Alceste or Monsieur Jourdain
—is criticizing the actual ; the reference to the
actual world is more direct. And having a more
tenuous reference, the work of Jonson is much less
directly satirical.

This leads us to the question of Humours.
Largely on the evidence of the two Humour plays,
it is sometimes assumed that Jonson is occupied

with types ; typical exaggerations, or exaggerations of type. The Humour definition, the expressed intention of Jonson, may be satisfactory for these two plays. *Every Man in his Humour* is the first mature work of Jonson, and the student of Jonson must study it ; but it is not the play in which Jonson found his genius : it is the last of his plays to read first. If one reads *Volpone*, and after that re-reads the *Jew of Malta* ; then returns to Jonson and reads *Bartholomew Fair*, *The Alchemist*, *Epicœne* and *The Devil is an Ass*, and finally *Catiline*, it is possible to arrive at a fair opinion of the poet and the dramatist.

The Humour, even at the beginning, is not a type, as in Marston's satire, but a simplified and somewhat distorted individual with a typical mania. In the later work, the Humour definition quite fails to account for the total effect produced. The characters of Shakespeare are such as might exist in different circumstances than those in which Shakespeare sets them. The latter appear to be those which extract from the characters the most intense and interesting realization ; but that realization has not exhausted their possibilities. Volpone's life, on the other hand, is bounded by the scene in which it is played ; in fact, the life is the life of the scene and is derivatively the life of Volpone ; the life of the character is inseparable from the life of the drama. This is not dependence upon a background, or upon a substratum of fact. The emotional effect is single and simple. Whereas in Shakespeare the effect is due to the way in which the characters *act upon* one another, in Jonson it is given by the way in which the characters *fit in* with each other. The artistic result of *Volpone* is not due to any effect that Volpone, Mosca, Corvino, Corbaccio, Voltore have upon each other, but simply to their combination into a whole. And these figures are not personifications of passions; separately, they have not even that reality, they are constituents. It is a similar indication of Jonson's method that you can hardly pick out a line of Jonson's and say confidently that it is great poetry; but there are many extended passages to which you cannot deny that honour.

> I will have all my beds blown up, not stuft;
> Down is too hard; and then, mine oval room
> Fill'd with such pictures as Tiberius took
> From Elephantis, and dull Aretine
> But coldly imitated. Then, my glasses
> Cut in more subtle angles, to disperse
> And multiply the figures, as I walk. . . .

Jonson is the legitimate heir of Marlowe. The man who wrote, in *Volpone*:

> for thy love,
> In varying figures, I would have contended
> With the blue Proteus, or the hornèd flood. . . .

and

> See, a carbuncle
> May put out both the eyes of our Saint Mark;
> A diamond would have bought Lollia Paulina,
> When she came in like star-light, hid with jewels. . . .

is related to Marlowe as a poet; and if Marlowe is a poet, Jonson is also. And, if Jonson's comedy is a comedy of humours, then Marlowe's tragedy, a large part of it, is a tragedy of humours. But Jonson has too exclusively been considered as the typical representative of a point of view toward comedy. He has suffered from his great reputation as a critic and theorist, from the effects of his intelligence. We have been taught to think of him as the man, the dictator (confusedly in our minds with his later namesake), as the literary politician impressing his views upon a generation; we are offended by the constant reminder of his scholarship. We forget the comedy in the humours, and the serious artist in the scholar. Jonson has suffered in public opinion, as anyone must suffer who is forced to talk about his art.

If you examine the first hundred lines or more of *Volpone* the verse appears to be in the manner of Marlowe, more deliberate, more mature, but without Marlowe's inspiration. It looks like mere "rhetoric," certainly not "deeds and language such as men do use"! It appears to us, in fact, forced and flagitious bombast. That it is not "rhetoric," or at least not vicious rhetoric, we do not know until we are able to review the whole play. For the consistent maintenance of this manner conveys in the end an effect not of verbosity, but of bold, even shocking and terrifying directness. We have difficulty in saying exactly what produces this simple and single effect. It is not in any ordinary way due to management of intrigue. Jonson employs immense dramatic constructive skill: it is not so much skill in plot as skill in doing without a plot. He never manipulates as complicated a plot as that of *The Merchant of Venice*; he has in his best plays nothing like the intrigue of Restoration comedy. In *Bartholomew Fair* it is hardly a plot at all; the marvel of the play is the bewildering rapid chaotic action of the fair; it is the fair itself, not anything that happens to take place in the fair. In *Volpone*, or *The Alchemist*, or *The Silent Woman*, the plot is enough to keep the players in motion; it is rather an "action" than a plot. The plot does not hold the play together; what holds the play together is a unity of inspiration that radiates into plot and personages alike.

We have attempted to make more precise the sense in which it was said that Jonson's work is "of the surface"; carefully avoiding the word "superficial." For there is work contemporary with Jonson's which is superficial in a pejorative sense in which the word cannot be applied to Jonson—the work of Beaumont and Fletcher. If we look at the work of Jonson's great contemporaries, Shakespeare, and also Donne and Webster and Tourneur (and sometimes Middleton), have a depth, a third dimension, as Mr. Gregory Smith rightly calls it, which Jonson's work has not. Their words have often a network of tentacular roots reaching down to the deepest terrors and desires. Jonson's most certainly have not; but in Beaumont and Fletcher we may think that at times we find it. Looking closer, we discover that the blossoms of Beaumont and Fletcher's imagination draw no sustenance from the soil, but are cut and slightly withered flowers stuck into sand.

> Wilt thou, hereafter, when they talk of me,
> As thou shalt hear nothing but infamy,
> Remember some of these things ? . . .
> I pray thee, do ; for thou shalt never see me so again.
>
> Hair woven in many a curious warp,
> Able in endless error to enfold
> The wandering soul ; . . .

Detached from its context, this looks like the verse of the greater poets ; just as lines of Jonson, detached from their context, look like inflated or empty fustian. But the evocative quality of the verse of Beaumont and Fletcher depends upon a clever appeal to emotions and associations which they have not themselves grasped ; it is hollow. It is superficial with a vacuum behind it ; the superficies of Jonson is solid. It is what it is ; it does not pretend to be another thing. But it is so very conscious and deliberate that we must look with eyes alert to the whole before we apprehend the significance of any part. We cannot call a man's work superficial when it is the creation of a world ; a man cannot be accused of dealing superficially with the world which he himself has created ; the superficies *is* the world. Jonson's characters conform to the logic of the emotions of their world. It is a world like Lobatchevsky's ; the worlds created by artists like Jonson are like systems of non-Euclidean geometry. They are not fancy, because they have a logic of their own ; and this logic illuminates the actual world, because it gives us a new point of view from which to inspect it.

A writer of power and intelligence, Jonson endeavoured to promulgate, as a formula and programme of reform, what he chose to do himself ; and he not unnaturally laid down in abstract theory what is in reality a personal point of view. And it is in the end of no value to discuss Jonson's theory and practice unless we recognize and seize this point of view, which escapes the formulae, and which is what makes his plays worth reading. Jonson behaved as the great creative mind that he was : he created his own world, a world from which his followers, as well as the dramatists who were trying to do something wholly different, are excluded. Remembering this, we turn to Mr. Gregory Smith's objection—that Jonson's characters lack the third dimension, have no life out of the theatrical existence in which they appear— and demand an inquest. The objection implies that the characters are purely the work of intellect, or the result of superficial observation of a world which is faded or mildewed. It implies that the characters are lifeless. But if we dig beneath the theory, beneath the observation, beneath the deliberate drawing and the theatrical and dramatic elaboration, there is discovered a kind of power, animating Volpone, Busy, Fitzdottrel, the literary ladies of *Epicœne*, even Bobadil, which comes from below the intellect, and for which no theory of humours will account. And it is the same kind of power which vivifies Trimalchio, and Panurge, and some but not all of the " comic " characters of Dickens. The fictive life of this kind is not to be circumscribed by a reference to " comedy " or to " farce " ; it is not exactly the kind of life which informs the characters of Molière or that which informs those of Marivaux—two writers who were, besides, doing something quite different the one from the other. But it is something which distinguishes Barabas from Shylock, Epicure Mammon from Falstaff, Faustus from—if you will—Macbeth ; Marlowe and Jonson from Shakespeare and the Shakespearians, Webster, and Tourneur. It is not merely Humours : for neither Volpone nor Mosca is a humour. No theory of humours could account for Jonson's best plays or the best characters in them. We want to know at what point the comedy of humours passes into a work of art, and why Jonson is not Brome.

The creation of a work of art, we will say the creation of a character in a drama, consists in the process of transfusion of the personality, or, in a deeper sense, the life, of the author into the character. This is a very different matter from the orthodox creation in one's own image. The ways in which the passions and desires of the creator may be satisfied in the work of art are complex and devious. In a painter they may take the form of a predilection for certain colours, tones, or light-ings ; in a writer the original impulse may be even more strangely transmuted. Now, we may say with Mr. Gregory Smith that Falstaff or a score of Shakespeare's characters have a "third dimension" that Jonson's have not. This will mean, not that Shakespeare's spring from the feelings or imagina-tion and Jonson's from the intellect or invention ; they have equally an emotional source ; but that Shakespeare's represent a more complex tissue of feelings and desires, as well as a more supple, a more susceptible temperament. Falstaff is not only the roast Malmesbury ox with the pudding in his belly ; he also "grows old," and, finally, his nose is as sharp as a pen. He was perhaps the *satisfaction* of more, and of more complicated feelings ; and perhaps he was, as the great tragic characters must have been, the offspring of deeper, less apprehensible feelings : deeper, but not necessarily stronger or more intense, than those of Jonson. It is obvious that the spring of the difference is not the difference between feeling and thought, or superior insight, superior perception, on the part of Shakespeare, but his suceptibility to a greater range of emotion, and emotion deeper and more obscure. But his characters are no more "alive" than are the characters of Jonson.

The world they live in is a larger one. But small worlds—the worlds which artists create—do not differ only in magnitude ; if they are complete worlds, drawn to scale in every part, they differ

in kind also. And Jonson's world has this scale.
His type of personality found its relief in something
falling under the category of burlesque or farce—
though when you are dealing with a *unique* world,
like his, these terms fail to appease the desire for
definition. It is not, at all events, the farce of
Molière: the latter is more analytic, more an
intellectual redistribution. It is not defined by
the word "satire." Jonson poses as a satirist.
But satire like Jonson's is great in the end not by
hitting off its object, but by creating it; the satire
is merely the means which leads to the æsthetic
result, the impulse which projects a new world into
a new orbit. In *Every Man in his Humour* there
is a neat, a very neat, comedy of humours. In
discovering and proclaiming in this play the new
genre Jonson was simply recognizing, unconsciously,
the route which opened out in the proper direction
for his instincts. His characters are and remain,
like Marlowe's, simplified characters; but the simplification does not consist in the dominance of a
particular humour or monomania. That is a very
superficial account of it. The simplification consists largely in reduction of detail, in the seizing of
aspects relevant to the relief of an emotional
impulse which remains the same for that character,
in making the character conform to a particular
setting. This stripping is essential to the art,
to which is also essential a flat distortion in the
drawing; it is an art of caricature, of great caricature, like Marlowe's. It is a great caricature, which

is beautiful ; and a great humour, which is serious. The " world " of Jonson is sufficiently large ; it is a world of poetic imagination ; it is sombre. He did not get the third dimension, but he was not trying to get it.

If we approach Jonson with less frozen awe of his learning, with a clearer understanding of his " rhetoric " and its applications, if we grasp the fact that the knowledge required of the reader is not archæology but knowledge of Jonson, we can derive not only instruction in non-Euclidean humanity—but enjoyment. We can even apply him, be aware of him as a part of our literary inheritance craving further expression. Of all the dramatists of his time, Jonson is probably the one whom the present age would find the most sympathetic, if it knew him. There is a brutality, a lack of sentiment, a polished surface, a handling of large bold designs in brilliant colours, which ought to attract about three thousand people in London and elsewhere. At least, if we had a contemporary Shakespeare and a contemporary Jonson, it would be the Jonson who would arouse the enthusiasm of the intelligentsia ! Though he is saturated in literature, he never sacrifices the theatrical qualities—theatrical in the most favourable sense—to literature or to the study of character. His work is a titanic show. But Jonson's masques, an important part of his work, are neglected ; our flaccid culture lets shows and literature fade, but prefers faded literature to faded shows. There are hundreds of people who

have read *Comus* to ten who have read the *Masque
of Blackness*. *Comus* contains fine poetry, and
poetry exemplifying some merits to which Jonson's
masque poetry cannot pretend. Nevertheless,
Comus is the death of the masque ; it is the transition of a form of art—even of a form which existed
for but a short generation—into " literature,"
literature cast in a form which has lost its application. Even though *Comus* was a masque at Ludlow
Castle, Jonson had, what Milton came perhaps too
late to have, a sense for living art ; his art was
applied. The masques can still be read, and with
pleasure, by anyone who will take the trouble—
a trouble which in this part of Jonson is, indeed,
a study of antiquities—to imagine them in action,
displayed with the music, costumes, dances, and
the scenery of Inigo Jones. They are additional
evidence that Jonson had a fine sense of form, of
the purpose for which a particular form is intended ;
evidence that he was a literary artist even more
than he was a man of letters.

PHILIP MASSINGER

I

MASSINGER has been more fortunately and more fairly judged than several of his greater contemporaries. Three critics have done their best by him : the notes of Coleridge exemplify Coleridge's fragmentary and fine perceptions ; the essay of Leslie Stephen is a piece of formidable destructive analysis ; and the essay of Swinburne is Swinburne's criticism at its best. None of these, probably, has put Massinger finally and irrefutably into a place.

English criticism is inclined to argue or persuade rather than to state ; and, instead of forcing the subject to expose himself, these critics have left in their work an undissolved residuum of their own good taste, which, however impeccable, is something that requires our faith. The principles which animate this taste remain unexplained. Mr. Cruickshank's book is a work of scholarship ; and the advantage of good scholarship is that it presents us with evidence which is an invitation to the critical faculty of the reader : it bestows a method, rather than a judgment.

It is difficult—it is perhaps the supreme difficulty

of criticism—to make the facts generalize themselves ; but Mr. Cruickshank at least presents us
with facts which are capable of generalization.'
This is a service of value ; and it is therefore wholly
a compliment to the author to say that his append-
ices are as valuable as the essay itself.

The sort of labour to which Mr. Cruickshank has
devoted himself is one that professed critics ought
more willingly to undertake.   It is an important part
of criticism, more important than any mere expression of opinion.   To understand Elizabethan drama
it is necessary to study a dozen playwrights at once,
to dissect with all care the complex growth, to
ponder collaboration to the utmost line.   Reading
Shakespeare and several of his contemporaries is
pleasure enough, perhaps all the pleasure possible,
for most.   But if we wish to consummate and
refine this pleasure by understanding it, to distil
the last drop of it, to press and press the essence
of each author, to apply exact measurement to
our own sensations, then we must compare ; and
we cannot compare without parcelling the threads
of authorship and influence.   We must employ
Mr. Cruickshank's judgments ;   and perhaps the
most important judgment to which he has committed himself is this :

Massinger, in his grasp of stagecraft, his flexible metre,
his desire in the sphere of ethics to exploit both vice and
virtue, is typical of an age which had much culture, but
which, without being exactly corrupt, lacked moral fibre.

Here, in fact, is our text : to elucidate this sentence would be to account for Massinger. We begin vaguely with good taste, by a recognition that Massinger is inferior : can we trace this inferiority, dissolve it, and have left any element of merit ?

We turn first to the parallel quotations from Massinger and Shakespeare collocated by Mr. Cruickshank to make manifest Massinger's indebtedness. One of the surest of tests is the way in which a poet borrows. Immature poets imitate ; mature poets steal ; bad poets deface what they take, and good poets make it into something better, or at least something different. The good poet welds his theft into a whole of feeling which is unique, utterly different from that from which it was torn ; the bad poet throws it into something which has no cohesion. A good poet will usually borrow from authors remote in time, or alien in language, or diverse in interest. Chapman borrowed from Seneca ; Shakespeare and Webster from Montaigne. The two great followers of Shakespeare, Webster and Tourneur, in their mature work do not borrow from him ; he is too close to them to be of use to them in this way. Massinger, as Mr. Cruickshank shows, borrows from Shakespeare a good deal. Let us profit by some of the quotations with which he has provided us—

Massinger : Can I call back yesterday, with all their aids
        That bow unto my sceptre ? or restore
        My mind to that tranquillity and peace
        It then enjoyed ?

Shakespeare : Not poppy, nor mandragora,
      Nor all the drowsy syrops of the world
      Shall ever medecine thee to that sweet sleep
      Which thou owedst yesterday.

Massinger's is a general rhetorical question, the language just and pure, but colourless. Shakespeare's has particular significance ; and the adjective " drowsy " and the verb " medecine " infuse a precise vigour. This is, on Massinger's part, an echo, rather than an imitation or a plagiarism— the basest, because least conscious form of borrowing. " Drowsy syrop " is a condensation of meaning frequent in Shakespeare, but rare in Massinger.

Massinger : Thou didst not borrow of Vice her indirect,
      Crooked, and abject means.

Shakespeare : God knows, my son,
      By what by-paths and indirect crook'd ways
      I met this crown.

Here, again, Massinger gives the general forensic statement, Shakespeare the particular image. " Indirect crook'd " is forceful in Shakespeare ; a mere pleonasm in Massinger. " Crook'd ways " is a metaphor ; Massinger's phrase only the ghost of a metaphor.

Massinger : And now, in the evening,
      When thou shoud'st pass with honour to thy rest,
      Wilt thou fall like a meteor ?

Shakespeare : I shall fall
      Like a bright exhalation in the evening,
      And no man see me more.

Here the lines of Massinger have their own beauty. Still, a " bright exhalation " appears to the eye and makes us catch our breath in the evening ; " meteor " is a dim simile ; the word is worn.

Massinger : What you deliver to me shall be lock'd up
In a strong cabinet, of which you yourself
Shall keep the key.

Shakespeare : 'Tis in my memory locked,
And you yourself shall keep the key of it.

In the preceding passage Massinger had squeezed his simile to death, here he drags it round the city at his heels ; and how swift Shakespeare's figure is ! We may add two more passages, not given by our commentator ; here the model is Webster. They occur on the same page, an artless confession.

Here he comes,
His nose held up ; he hath something in the wind,

is hardly comparable to " the Cardinal lifts up his nose like a foul porpoise before a storm," and when we come upon

as tann'd galley-slaves
Pay such as do redeem them from the oar

it is unnecessary to turn up the great lines in the *Duchess of Malfi*. Massinger fancied this galley-slave ; for he comes with his oar again in the *Bondman*—

Never did galley-slave shake off his chains,
Or looked on his redemption from the oar. . . .

Now these are mature plays ; and the *Roman Actor*
(from which we have drawn the two previous
extracts) is said to have been the preferred play of
its author.

We may conclude directly from these quotations
that Massinger's feeling for language had out-
stripped his feeling for things ; that his eye and his
vocabulary were not in co-operation. One of the
greatest distinctions of several of his elder contemporaries—we name Middleton, Webster, Tourneur—is a gift for combining, for fusing into a single
phrase, two or more diverse impressions.

> . . . in her strong toil of grace

of Shakespeare is such a fusion ; the metaphor
identifies itself with what suggests it ; the resultant
is one and is unique—

> Does the silk worm *expend* her *yellow labours* ? . . .
> Why does yon fellow *falsify highways*
> And lays his life between the judge's lips
> To *refine* such a one ? keeps horse and men
> To *beat their valours* for her ?
>
> Let the common sewer take it from distinction. . . .
> Lust and forgetfulness have been amongst us. . . .

These lines of Tourneur and of Middleton exhibit
that perpetual slight alteration of language, words
perpetually juxtaposed in new and sudden combinations, meanings perpetually *eingeschachtelt* into
meanings, which evidences a very high development
of the senses, a development of the English language

which we have perhaps never equalled. And, indeed, with the end of Chapman, Middleton, Webster, Tourneur, Donne we end a period when the intellect was immediately at the tips of the senses. Sensation became word and word was sensation. The next period is the period of Milton (though still with a Marvell in it); and this period is initiated by Massinger.

It is not that the word becomes less exact. Massinger is, in a wholly eulogistic sense, choice and correct. And the decay of the senses is not inconsistent with a greater sophistication of language. But every vital development in language is a development of feeling as well. The verse of Shakespeare and the major Shakespearean dramatists is an innovation of this kind, a true mutation of species. The verse practised by Massinger is a different verse from that of his predecessors ; but it is not a development based on, or resulting from, a new way of feeling. On the contrary, it seems to lead us away from feeling altogether.

We mean that Massinger must be placed as much at the beginning of one period as at the end of another. A certain Boyle, quoted by Mr. Cruickshank, says that Milton's blank verse owes much to the study of Massinger's.

In the indefinable touches which make up the music of a verse [says Boyle], in the artistic distribution of pauses, and in the unerring choice and grouping of just those words which strike the ear as the perfection of harmony, there are, if we leave Cyril Tourneur's *Atheist's*

Tragedy out of the question, only two masters in the drama, Shakespeare in his latest period and Massinger.

This Boyle must have had a singular ear to have preferred Tourneur's apprentice work to his *Revenger's Tragedy*, and one must think that he had never glanced at Ford. But though the appraisal be ludicrous, the praise is not undeserved. Mr. Cruickshank has given us an excellent example of Massinger's syntax—

> What though my father
> Writ man before he was so, and confirm'd it,
> By numbering that day no part of his life
> In which he did not service to his country;
> Was he to be free therefore from the laws
> And ceremonious form in your decrees ?
> Or else because he did as much as man
> In those three memorable overthrows,
> At Granson, Morat, Nancy, where his master,
> The warlike Charalois, with whose misfortunes
> I bear his name, lost treasure, men, and life,
> To be excused from payment of those sums
> Which (his own patrimony spent) his zeal
> To serve his country forced him to take up !

It is impossible to deny the masterly construction of this passage ; perhaps there is not one living poet who could do the like. It is impossible to deny the originality. The language is pure and correct, free from muddiness or turbidity. Massinger does not confuse metaphors, or heap them one upon another. He is lucid, though not easy. But if Massinger's age, " without being exactly corrupt, lacks moral fibre," Massinger's verse, without being exactly corrupt, suffers from cerebral anæmia. To say that an involved style is necessarily a bad style would be preposterous. But such a style should follow the involutions of a mode of perceiving, registering, and digesting impressions which is also involved. It is to be feared that the feeling of Massinger is simple and overlaid with received ideas. Had Massinger had a nervous system as refined as that of Middleton, Tourneur, Webster, or Ford, his style would be a triumph. But such a nature was not at hand, and Massinger precedes, not another Shakespeare, but Milton.

Massinger is, in fact, at a further remove from Shakespeare than that other precursor of Milton— John Fletcher. Fletcher was above all an opportunist, in his verse, in his momentary effects, never quite a pastiche ; in his structure ready to sacrifice everything to the single scene. To Fletcher, because he was more intelligent, less will be forgiven. Fletcher had a cunning guess at feelings, and betrayed them ; Massinger was unconscious and innocent. As an artisan of the theatre he is not inferior to Fletcher, and his best tragedies have an honester unity that *Bonduca*. But the unity is superficial. In the *Roman Actor* the development of parts is out of all proportion to the central theme ; in the *Unnatural Combat*, in spite of the deft handling of suspense and the quick shift from climax to a new suspense, the first part of the play is the hatred of Malefort for his son and the second part is his passion for his daughter. It is theatrical skill, not an artistic conscience arranging emotions, that holds the two parts together. In the *Duke of Milan* the appearance of Sforza at the Court of his conqueror only delays the action, or rather breaks the emotional rhythm. And we have named three of Massinger's best.

A dramatist who so skilfully welds together parts which have no reason for being together, who fabricates plays so well knit and so remote from unity, we should expect to exhibit the same synthetic cunning in character. Mr. Cruickshank, Coleridge, and Leslie Stephen are pretty well agreed that Massinger is no master of characterization. You can, in fact, put together heterogeneous parts to form a lively play ; but a character, to be living, must be conceived from some emotional unity. A character is not to be composed of scattered observations of human nature, but of parts which are felt together. Hence it is that although Massinger's failure to draw a moving character is no greater than his failure to make a whole play, and probably springs from the same defective sensitiveness, yet the failure in character is more conspicuous and more disastrous. A " living " character is not necessarily " true to life." It is a person whom we can see and hear, whether he be true or false to human nature as we know it. What the creator of character needs is not so much knowledge of motives as keen sensibility ; the dramatist need not understand people ; but he must be exceptionally aware of them. This awareness was not given to Massinger. He inherits the traditions of conduct, female chastity, hymeneal sanctity, the fashion of honour, without either criticizing or informing them from his own experience. In the earlier drama these conventions are merely a framework, or an alloy necessary for working the metal ; the metal itself consisted of unique emotions resulting inevitably from the circumstances, resulting or inhering as inevitably as the properties of a chemical compound. Middleton's heroine, for instance, in the *Changeling*, exclaims in the well-known words—

> Why, 'tis impossible thou canst be so wicked,
> To shelter such a cunning cruelty
> To make his death the murderer of my honour !

The word " honour " in such a situation is out of date, but the emotion of Beatrice at that moment, given the conditions, is as permanent and substantial as anything in human nature. The emotion of Othello in Act v. is the emotion of a man who discovers that the worst part of his own soul has been exploited by some one more clever than he ; it is this emotion carried by the writer to a very high degree of intensity. Even in so late and so decayed a drama as that of Ford, the framework of emotions and morals of the time is only the vehicle for statements of feeling which are unique and imperishable : Ford's and Ford's only.

What may be considered corrupt or decadent in the morals of Massinger is not an alteration or diminution in morals ; it is simply the disappearance of all the personal and real emotions which this

morality supported and into which it introduced a
kind of order. As soon as the emotions disappear
the morality which ordered it appears hideous.
Puritanism itself became repulsive only when it
appeared as the survival of a restraint after the
feelings which it restrained had gone. When
Massinger's ladies resist temptation they do not
appear to undergo any important emotion; they
merely know what is expected of them; they
manifest themselves to us as lubricious prudes.
Any age has its conventions; and any age might
appear absurd when its conventions get into the
hands of a man like Massinger—a man, we mean,
of so exceptionally superior a literary talent as
Massinger's, and so paltry an imagination. The
Elizabethan morality was an important convention; important because it was not consciously of
one social class alone, because it provided a framework for emotions to which all classes could respond,
and it hindered no feeling. It was not hypocritical,
and it did not suppress; its dark corners are
haunted by the ghosts of Mary Fitton and perhaps
greater. It is a subject which has not been sufficiently investigated. Fletcher and Massinger rendered it ridiculous; not by not believing it, but
because they were men of great talents who could
not vivify it; because they could not fit into it
passionate, complete human characters.

The tragedy of Massinger is interesting chiefly
according to the definition given before; the highest
degree of verbal excellence compatible with the most

rudimentary development of the senses. Massinger succeeds better in something which is not tragedy; in the romantic comedy. *A Very Woman* deserves all the praise that Swinburne, with his almost unerring gift for selection, has bestowed upon it. The probable collaboration of Fletcher had the happiest result; for certainly that admirable comic personage, the tipsy Borachia, is handled with more humour than we expect of Massinger. It is a play which would be enjoyable on the stage. The form, however, of romantic comedy is itself inferior and decadent. There is an inflexibility about the poetic drama which is by no means a matter of classical, or neoclassical, or pseudo-classical law. The poetic drama might develop forms highly different from those of Greece or England, India or Japan. Conceded the utmost freedom, the romantic drama would yet remain inferior. The poetic drama must have an emotional unity, let the emotion be whatever you like. It must have a dominant tone; and if this be strong enough, the most heterogeneous emotions may be made to reinforce it. The romantic comedy is a skilful concoction of inconsistent emotion, a *revue* of emotion. *A Very Woman* is surpassingly well plotted. The debility of romantic drama does not depend upon extravagant setting, or preposterous events, or inconceivable coincidences; all these might be found in a serious tragedy or comedy. It consists in an internal incoherence of feelings, a concatenation of emotions which signifies nothing.

From this type of play, so eloquent of emotional disorder, there was no swing back of the pendulum. Changes never come by a simple reinfusion into the form which the life has just left. The romantic drama was not a new form. Massinger dealt not with emotions so much as with the social abstractions of emotions, more generalized and therefore more quickly and easily interchangeable within the confines of a single action. He was not guided by direct communications through the nerves. Romantic drama tended, accordingly, toward what is sometimes called the " typical," but which is not the truly typical ; for the *typical* figure in a drama is always particularized—an individual. The tendency of the romantic drama was toward a form which continued it in removing its more conspicuous vices, was toward a more severe external order. This form was the Heroic Drama. We look into Dryden's " Essay on Heroic Plays,"and we find that " love and valour ought to be the subject of an heroic poem." Massinger, in his destruction of the old drama, had prepared the way for Dryden. The intellect had perhaps exhausted the old conventions. It was not able to supply the impoverishment of feeling.

Such are the reflections aroused by an examination of some of Massinger's plays in the light of Mr. Cruickshank's statement that Massinger's age " had much more culture, but, without being exactly corrupt, lacked moral fibre." The statement may be supported. In order to fit into our estimate of Massinger the two admirable comedies—*A New Way to Pay Old Debts* and *The City Madam*—a more extensive research would be required than is possible within our limits.

II

Massinger's tragedy may be summarized for the unprepared reader as being very dreary. It is dreary, unless one is prepared by a somewhat extensive knowledge of his livelier contemporaries to grasp without fatigue precisely the elements in it which are capable of giving pleasure ; or unless one is incited by a curious interest in versification. In comedy, however, Massinger was one of the few masters in the language. He was a master in a comedy which is serious, even sombre ; and in one aspect of it there are only two names to mention with his : those of Marlowe and Jonson. In comedy, as a matter of fact, a greater variety of methods were discovered and employed than in tragedy. The method of Kyd, as developed by Shakespeare, was the standard for English tragedy down to Otway and to Shelley. But both individual temperament, and varying epochs, made more play with comedy. The comedy of Lyly is one thing ; that of Shakespeare, followed by Beaumont and Fletcher, is another ; and that of Middleton is a third. And Massinger, while he has his own comedy, is nearer to Marlowe and Jonson than to any of these.

Massinger was, in fact, as a comic writer, fortunate in the moment at which he wrote. His comedy is transitional ; but it happens to be one of those transitions which contain some merit not anticipated by predecessors or refined upon by later writers. The comedy of Jonson is nearer to caricature ; that of Middleton a more photographic delineation of low life. Massinger is nearer to Restoration comedy, and more like his contemporary, Shirley, in assuming a certain social level, certain distinctions of class, as a postulate of his comedy. This resemblance to later comedy is also the important point of difference between Massinger and earlier comedy. But Massinger's comedy differs just as widely from the comedy of manners proper ; he is closer to that in his romantic drama—in *A Very Woman*—than in *A New Way to Pay Old Debts* ; in his comedy his interest is not in the follies of love-making or the absurdities of social pretence, but in the unmasking of villainy. Just as the Old Comedy of Molière differs in principle from the New Comedy of Marivaux, so the Old Comedy of Massinger differs from the New Comedy of his contemporary Shirley. And as in France, so in England, the more farcical comedy was the more serious. Massinger's great comic rogues, Sir Giles Overreach and Luke Frugal, are members of the large English family which includes Barabas and Sir Epicure Mammon, and from which Sir Tunbelly Clumsy claims descent.

What distinguishes Massinger from Marlowe and Jonson is in the main an inferiority. The greatest comic characters of these two dramatists are slight work in comparison with Shakespeare's best—

Falstaff has a third dimension and Epicure Mammon has only two. But this slightness is part of the nature of the art which Jonson practised, a smaller art than Shakespeare's. The inferiority of Massinger to Jonson is an inferiority, not of one type of art to another, but within Jonson's type. It is a simple deficiency. Marlowe's and Jonson's comedies were a view of life ; they were, as great literature is, the transformation of a personality into a personal work of art, their lifetime's work, long or short. Massinger is not simply a smaller personality : his personality hardly exists. He did not, out of his own personality, build a world of art, as Shakespeare and Marlowe and Jonson built.

In the fine pages which Remy de Gourmont devotes to Flaubert in his *Problème du Style*, the great critic declares :

La vie est un dépouillement. Le but de l'activité propre de l'homme est de nettoyer sa personnalité, de la laver de toutes les souillures qu'y déposa l'éducation, de la dégager de toutes les empreintes qu'y laissèrent nos admirations adolescentes ;

and again :

Flaubert incorporait toute sa sensibilité à ses œuvres. . . . Hors de ses livres, où il se transvasait goutte à goutte, jusqu'à la lie, Flaubert est fort peu intéressant. . . .

Of Shakespeare notably, of Jonson less, of Marlowe (and of Keats to the term of life allowed him), one can say that they *se transvasaient goutte à goutte* ; and

in England, which has produced a prodigious
number of men of genius and comparatively few
works of art, there are not many writers of whom
one can say it. Certainly not of Massinger. A
brilliant master of technique, he was not, in this
profound sense, an artist. And so we come to
inquire how, if this is so, he could have written
two great comedies. We shall probably be obliged
to conclude that a large part of their excellence is,
in some way which should be defined, fortuitous ;
and that therefore they are, however remarkable,
not works of perfect art.

This objection raised by Leslie Stephen to Massinger's method of revealing a villain has great
cogency ; but I am inclined to believe that the
cogency is due to a somewhat different reason from
that which Leslie Stephen assigns. His statement is
too *apriorist* to be quite trustworthy. There is no
reason why a comedy or a tragedy villain should not
declare himself, and in as long a period as the author
likes ; but the sort of villain who may run on in this
way is a simple villain (simple not *simpliste*).
Barabas and Volpone can declare their character,
because they have no inside ; appearance and reality
are coincident ; they are forces in particular directions. Massinger's two villains are not simple.
Giles Overreach is essentially a great force directed
upon small objects ; a great force, a small mind ;
the terror of a dozen parishes instead of the conqueror
of a world. The force is misapplied, attenuated,
thwarted, by the man's vulgarity : he is a great

man of the City, without fear, but with the most
abject awe of the aristocracy. He is accordingly
not simple, but a product of a certain civilization,
and he is not wholly conscious. His monologues
are meant to be, not what he thinks he is, but what
he really is : and yet they are not the truth about
him, and he himself certainly does not know the
truth. To declare himself, therefore, is impossible.

> Nay, when my ears are pierced with widows' cries,
> And undone orphans wash with tears my threshold,
> I only think what 'tis to have my daughter
> Right honourable ; and 'tis a powerful charm
> Makes me insensible of remorse, or pity,
> Or the least sting of conscience.

This is the wrong note. Elsewhere we have the
right :

> Thou art a fool ;
> In being out of office, I am out of danger ;
> Where, if I were a justice, besides the trouble,
> I might or out of wilfulness, or error,
> Run myself finely into a praemunire,
> And so become a prey to the informer,
> No, I'll have none of't ; 'tis enough I keep
> Greedy at my devotion : so he serve
> My purposes, let him hang, or damn, I care not . . .

And how well tuned, well modulated, here, the diction ! The man is audible and visible. But from
passages like the first we may be permitted to infer
that Massinger was unconscious of trying to develop
a different kind of character from any that Marlowe
or Jonson had invented.

Luke Frugal, in *The City Madam*, is not so great a

6

character as Sir Giles Overreach. But Luke Frugal just misses being almost the greatest of all hypocrites. His humility in the first act of the play is more than half real. The error in his portraiture is not the extravagant hocus-pocus of supposed Indian necromancers by which he is so easily duped, but the premature disclosure of villainy in his temptation of the two apprentices of his brother. But for this, he would be a perfect chameleon of circumstance. Here, again, we feel that Massinger was conscious only of inventing a rascal of the old simpler farce type. But the play is not a farce, in the sense in which *The Jew of Malta*, *The Alchemist*, *Bartholomew Fair* are farces. Massinger had not the personality to create great farce, and he was too serious to invent trivial farce. The ability to perform that slight distortion of *all* the elements in the world of a play or a story, so that this world is complete in itself, which was given to Marlowe and Jonson (and to Rabelais) and which is prerequisite to great farce, was denied to Massinger. On the other hand, his temperament was more closely related to theirs than to that of Shirley or the Restoration wits. His two comedies therefore occupy a place by themselves. His ways of thinking and feeling isolate him from both the Elizabethan and the later Caroline mind. He might almost have been a great realist ; he is killed by conventions which were suitable for the preceding literary generation, but not for his. Had Massinger been a greater man, a man of more intellectual courage, the current of English literature immediately after him might have taken a different course. The defect is precisely a defect of personality. He is not, however, the only man of letters who, at the moment when a new view of life is wanted, has looked at life through the eyes of his predecessors, and only at manners through his own.

SWINBURNE AS POET

IT is a question of some nicety to decide how much must be read of any particular poet. And it is not a question merely of the size of the poet. There are some poets whose every line has unique value. There are others who can be taken by a few poems universally agreed upon. There are others who need be read only in selections, but what selections are read will not very much matter. Of Swinburne, we should like to have the *Atalanta* entire, and a volume of selections which should certainly contain *The Leper, Laus Veneris* and *The Triumph of Time*. It ought to contain many more, but there is perhaps no other single poem which it would be an error to omit. A student of Swinburne will want to read one of the Stuart plays and dip into *Tristram of Lyonesse*. But almost no one, to-day, will wish to read the whole of Swinburne. It is not because Swinburne is voluminous ; certain poets, equally voluminous, must be read entire. The necessity and the difficulty of a selection are due to the peculiar nature of Swinburne's contribution, which, it is hardly too much to say, is of a very different kind from that of any other poet of equal reputation.

144

We may take it as undisputed that Swinburne did make a contribution ; that he did something that had not been done before, and that what he did will not turn out to be a fraud. And from that we may proceed to inquire what Swinburne's contribution was, and why, whatever critical solvents we employ to break down the structure of his verse, this contribution remains. The test is this : agreed that we do not (and I think that the present generation does not) greatly enjoy Swinburne, and agreed that (a more serious condemnation) at one period of our lives we did enjoy him and now no longer enjoy him ; nevertheless, the words which we use to state our grounds of dislike or indifference cannot be applied to Swinburne as they can to bad poetry. The words of condemnation are words which express his qualities. You may say " diffuse." But the diffuseness is essential ; had Swinburne practised greater concentration his verse would be, not better in the same kind, but a different thing. His diffuseness is one of his glories. That so little material as appears to be employed in *The Triumph of Time* should release such an amazing number of words, requires what there is no reason to call anything but genius. You could not condense *The Triumph of Time*. You could only leave out. And this would destroy the poem ; though no one stanza seems essential. Similarly, a considerable quantity—a volume of selections—is necessary to give the quality of Swinburne although there is perhaps no one poem essential in this selection.

If, then, we must be very careful in applying terms of censure, like " diffuse," we must be equally careful of praise.   " The beauty of Swinburne's verse is the sound," people say, explaining, " he had little visual imagination."   I am inclined to think that the word " beauty " is hardly to be used in connection with Swinburne's verse at all ; but in any case the beauty or effect of sound is neither that of music nor that of poetry which can be set to music. There is no reason why verse intended to be sung should not present a sharp visual image or convey an important intellectual meaning, for it supplements the music by another means of affecting the feelings. What we get in Swinburne is an expression by sound, which could not possibly associate itself with music. For what he gives is not images and ideas and music, it is one thing with a curious mixture of suggestions of all three.

Shall I come, if I swim ? wide are the waves, you see ;
Shall I come, if I fly, my dear Love, to thee ?

This is Campion, and an example of the kind of music that is not to be found in Swinburne.   It is an arrangement and choice of words which has a sound-value and at the same time a coherent comprehensible meaning, and the two things—the musical value and meaning—are two things, not one. But in Swinburne there is no *pure* beauty—no pure beauty of sound, or of image, or of idea.

Music, when soft voices die,
Vibrates in the memory ;

> Odours, when sweet violets sicken,
> Live within the sense they quicken.
>
> Rose leaves, when the rose is dead,
> Are heaped for the beloved's bed ;
> And so thy thoughts, when thou art gone,
> Love itself shall slumber on.

I quote from Shelley, because Shelley is supposed to be the master of Swinburne ; and because his song, like that of Campion, has what Swinburne has not—a beauty of music and a beauty of content ; and because it is clearly and simply expressed, with only two adjectives. Now, in Swinburne the meaning and the sound are one thing. He is concerned with the meaning of the word in a peculiar way : he employs, or rather " works," the word's meaning. And this is connected with an interesting fact about his vocabulary : he uses the most general word, because his emotion is never particular, never in direct line of vision, never focused ; it is emotion reinforced, not by intensification, but by expansion.

> There lived a singer in France of old
> By the tideless dolorous midland sea.
> In a land of sand and ruin and gold
> There shone one woman, and none but she.

You see that Provence is the merest point of diffusion here. Swinburne defines the place by the most general word, which has for him its own value. " Gold," " ruin," " dolorous " : it is not merely the sound that he wants, but the vague associations of idea that the words give him. He has not his eye on a particular place, as—

> Li ruscelletti che dei verdi colli
> Del Casentin discendon giuso in Arno . . .

It is, in fact, the word that gives him the thrill, not the object. When you take to pieces any verse of Swinburne, you find always that the object was not there—only the word. Compare

> Snowdrops that plead for pardon
> And pine for fright

with the daffodils that come before the swallow dares. The snowdrop of Swinburne disappears, the daffodil of Shakespeare remains. The swallow of Shakespeare remains in the verse in *Macbeth*; the bird of Wordsworth

> Breaking the silence of the seas

remains; the swallow of "Itylus" disappears. Compare, again, a chorus of *Atalanta* with a chorus from Athenian tragedy. The chorus of Swinburne is almost a parody of the Athenian : it is sententious, but it has not even the significance of commonplace.

> At least we witness of thee ere we die
> That these things are not otherwise, but thus. . . .

> Before the beginning of years
>   There came to the making of man
> Time with a gift of tears;
>   Grief with a glass that ran. . . .

This is not merely " music "; it is effective because it appears to be a tremendous statement, like statements made in our dreams; when we wake up we find that the " glass that ran " would do better for

time than for grief, and that the gift of tears would
be as appropriately bestowed by grief as by time.

It might seem to be intimated, by what has been
said, that the work of Swinburne can be shown to
be a sham, just as bad verse is a sham. It would
only be so if you could produce or suggest something
that it pretends to be and is not. The world of
Swinburne does not depend upon some other world
which it simulates ; it has the necessary completeness and self-sufficiency for justification and per-
manence. It is impersonal, and no one else could
have made it. The deductions are true to the postu-
lates. It is indestructible. None of the obvious
complaints that were or might have been brought
to bear upon the first *Poems and Ballads* holds good.
The poetry is not morbid, it is not erotic, it is not
destructive. These are adjectives which can be
applied to the material, the human feelings, which in
Swinburne's case do not exist. The morbidity is
not of human feeling but of language. Language in
a healthy state presents the object, is so close to the
object that the two are identified.

They are identified in the verse of Swinburne
solely because the object has ceased to exist, because
the meaning is merely the hallucination of meaning,
because language, uprooted, has adapted itself to an
independent life of atmospheric nourishment. In
Swinburne, for example, we see the word " weary "
flourishing in this way independent of the particular
and actual weariness of flesh or spirit. The bad poet
dwells partly in a world of objects and partly in a

world of words, and he never can get them to fit.
Only a man of genius could dwell so exclusively and
consistently among words as Swinburne. His language is not, like the language of bad poetry, dead.
It is very much alive, with this singular life of its
own. But the language which is more important to
us is that which is struggling to digest and express
new objects, new groups of objects, new feelings, new
aspects, as, for instance, the prose of Mr. James
Joyce or the earlier Conrad.

BLAKE

I

IF one follow Blake's mind through the several
stages of his poetic development it is impossible
to regard him as a naïf, a wild man, a wild pet for
the supercultivated. The strangeness is evaporated,
the peculiarity is seen to be the peculiarity of all
great poetry : something which is found (not everywhere) in Homer and Æschylus and Dante and
Villon, and profound and concealed in the work of
Shakespeare—and also in another form in Montaigne
and in Spinoza. It is merely a peculiar honesty,
which, in a world too frightened to be honest, is
peculiarly terrifying. It is an honesty against
which the whole world conspires, because it is un-
pleasant. Blake's poetry has the unpleasantness of
great poetry. Nothing that can be called morbid or
abnormal or perverse, none of the things which
exemplify the sickness of an epoch or a fashion, have
this quality ; only those things which, by some
extraordinary labour of simplification, exhibit the
essential sickness or strength of the human soul.
And this honesty never exists without great technical
accomplishment. The question about Blake the
man is the question of the circumstances that con-

curred to permit this honesty in his work, and what circumstances define its limitations. The favouring conditions probably include these two : that, being early apprenticed to a manual occupation, he was not compelled to acquire any other education in literature than he wanted, or to acquire it for any other reason than that he wanted it ; and that, being a humble engraver, he had no journalistic-social career open to him.

There was, that is to say, nothing to distract him from his interests or to corrupt these interests : neither the ambitions of parents or wife, nor the standards of society, nor the temptations of success ; nor was he exposed to imitation of himself or of anyone else. These circumstances—not his supposed inspired and untaught spontaneity—are what make him innocent. His early poems show what the poems of a boy of genius ought to show, immense power of assimilation. Such early poems are not, as usually supposed, crude attempts to do something beyond the boy's capacity ; they are, in the case of a boy of real promise, more likely to be quite mature and successful attempts to do something small. So with Blake, his early poems are technically admirable, and their originality is in an occasional rhythm. The verse of *Edward III* deserves study. But his affection for certain Elizabethans is not so surprising as his affinity with the very best work of his own century. He is very like Collins, he is very eighteenth century. The poem *Whether on Ida's shady brow* is eighteenth-century work ; the movement, the weight of it, the syntax, the choice of words—

> The *languid* strings do scarcely move !
> The sound is *forc'd*, the notes are few !

this is contemporary with Gray and Collins, it is the poetry of a language which has undergone the discipline of prose. Blake up to twenty is decidedly a traditional.

Blake's beginnings as a poet, then, are as normal as the beginnings of Shakespeare. His method of composition, in his mature work, is exactly like that of other poets. He has an idea (a feeling, an image), he develops it by accretion or expansion, alters his verse often, and hesitates often over the final choice.[1] The idea, of course, simply comes, but upon arrival it is subjected to prolonged manipulation. In the first phase Blake is concerned with verbal beauty ; in the second he becomes the apparent naïf, really the mature intelligence. It is only when the ideas become more automatic, come more freely and are less

---

[1] I do not know why M. Berger should say, without qualification, in his *William Blake : mysticisme et poésie*, that " son respect pour l'esprit qui soufflait en lui et qui dictait ses paroles l'empêchait de les corriger jamais." Dr. Sampson, in his Oxford Edition of Blake, gives us to understand that Blake believed much of his writing to be automatic, but observes that Blake's " meticulous care in composition is everywhere apparent in the poems preserved in rough draft . . . alteration on alteration, rearrangement after rearrangement, deletions, additions, and inversions. . . ."

manipulated, that we begin to suspect their origin, to suspect that they spring from a shallower source.

The Songs of Innocence and of Experience, and the poems from the Rossetti manuscript, are the poems of a man with a profound interest in human emotions, and a profound knowledge of them. The emotions are presented in an extremely simplified, abstract form. This form is one illustration of the eternal struggle of art against education, of the literary artist against the continuous deterioration of language.

It is important that the artist should be highly educated in his own art ; but his education is one that is hindered rather than helped by the ordinary processes of society which constitute education for the ordinary man. For these processes consist largely in the acquisition of impersonal ideas which obscure what we really are and feel, what we really want, and what really excites our interest. It is of course not the actual information acquired, but the conformity which the accumulation of knowledge is apt to impose, that is harmful. Tennyson is a very fair example of a poet almost wholly encrusted with parasitic opinion, almost wholly merged into his environment. Blake, on the other hand, knew what interested him, and he therefore presents only the essential, only, in fact, what can be presented, and need not be explained. And because he was not distracted, or frightened, or occupied in anything but exact statement, he understood. He was naked, and saw man naked, and from the centre of his own

crystal. To him there was no more reason why
Swedenborg should be absurd than Locke. He
accepted Swedenborg, and eventually rejected him,
for reasons of his own. He approached everything
with a mind unclouded by current opinions. There
was nothing of the superior person about him. This
makes him terrifying.

II

But if there was nothing to distract him from sin-
cerity there were, on the other hand, the dangers
to which the naked man is exposed. His philosophy,
like his visions, like his insight, like his technique,
was his own. And accordingly he was inclined to
attach more importance to it than an artist should ;
this is what makes him eccentric, and makes him
inclined to formlessness.

> But most through midnight streets I hear
> How the youthful harlot's curse
> Blasts the new-born infant's tear,
> And blights with plagues the marriage hearse,

is the naked vision ;

> Love seeketh only self to please,
> To bind another to its delight,
> Joys in another's loss of ease,
> And builds a Hell in Heaven's despite,

is the naked observation ; and *The Marriage of
Heaven and Hell* is naked philosophy, presented.
But Blake's occasional marriages of poetry and
philosophy are not so felicitous.

He who would do good to another must do it in Minute
    Particulars.
General Good is the plea of the scoundrel, hypocrite, and
    flatterer ;
For Art and Science cannot exist but in minutely organized
    particulars. . . .

One feels that the form is not well chosen. The
borrowed philosophy of Dante and Lucretius is
perhaps not so interesting, but it injures their form
less. Blake did not have that more Mediterranean
gift of form which knows how to borrow as Dante
borrowed his theory of the soul ; he must needs
create a philosophy as well as a poetry. A similar
formlessness attacks his draughtsmanship. The
fault is most evident, of course, in the longer poems
—or rather, the poems in which structure is important. You cannot create a very large poem without
introducing a more impersonal point of view, or
splitting it up into various personalities. But the
weakness of the long poems is certainly not that
they are too visionary, too remote from the world.
It is that Blake did not see enough, became too much
occupied with ideas.

We have the same respect for Blake's philosophy
(and perhaps for that of Samuel Butler) that we have
for an ingenious piece of home-made furniture : we
admire the man who has put it together out of the
odds and ends about the house. England has produced a fair number of these resourceful Robinson
Crusoes ; but we are not really so remote from the
Continent, or from our own past, as to be deprived of
the advantages of culture if we wish them.

We may speculate, for amusement, whether it would not have been beneficial to the north of Europe generally, and to Britain in particular, to have had a more continuous religious history. The local divinities of Italy were not wholly exterminated by Christianity, and they were not reduced to the dwarfish fate which fell upon our trolls and pixies. The latter, with the major Saxon deities, were perhaps no great loss in themselves, but they left an empty place ; and perhaps our mythology was further impoverished by the divorce from Rome. Milton's celestial and infernal regions are large but insufficiently furnished apartments filled by heavy conversation ; and one remarks about the Puritan mythology an historical thinness. And about Blake's supernatural territories, as about the supposed ideas that dwell there, we cannot help commenting on a certain meanness of culture. They illustrate the crankiness, the eccentricity, which frequently affects writers outside of the Latin traditions, and which such a critic as Arnold should certainly have rebuked. And they are not essential to Blake's inspiration.

Blake was endowed with a capacity for considerable understanding of human nature, with a remarkable and original sense of language and the music of language, and a gift of hallucinated vision. Had these been controlled by a respect for impersonal reason, for common sense, for the objectivity of science, it would have been better for him. What his genius required, and what it sadly lacked, was a framework of accepted and traditional ideas which would have prevented him from indulging in a philosophy of his own, and concentrated his attention upon the problems of the poet. Confusion of thought, emotion, and vision is what we find in such a work as *Also Sprach Zarathustra* ; it is eminently not a Latin virtue. The concentration resulting from a framework of mythology and theology and philosophy is one of the reasons why Dante is a classic, and Blake only a poet of genius. The fault is perhaps not with Blake himself, but with the environment which failed to provide what such a poet needed ; perhaps the circumstances compelled him to fabricate, perhaps the poet required the philosopher and mythologist ; although the conscious Blake may have been quite unconscious of the motives.

DANTE

M. PAUL VALÉRY, a writer for whom I have considerable respect, has placed in his most recent statement upon poetry a paragraph which seems to me of very doubtful validity. I have not seen the complete essay, and know the quotation only as it appears in a critical notice in the *Athenæum*, July 23, 1920 :

La philosophie, et même la morale tendirent à fuir les œuvres pour se placer dans les réflexions qui les précèdent. . . . Parler aujourd'hui de poésie philosophique (fût-ce en invoquant Alfred de Vigny, Leconte de Lisle, et quelques autres), c'est naivement confondre des conditions et des applications de l'esprit incompatibles entre elles. N'est-ce pas oublier que le but de celui qui spécule est de fixer ou de créer une notion— c'est-à-dire un *pouvoir* et un *instrument de pouvoir*, cependant que le poète moderne essaie de produire en nous un *état* et de porter cet état exceptionnel au point d'une jouissance parfaite. . . .

It may be that I do M. Valéry an injustice which I must endeavour to repair when I have the pleasure of reading his article entire. But the paragraph gives the impression of more than one error of analysis. In the first place, it suggests that conditions have changed, that "philosophical" poetry may once have been permissible, but that (perhaps owing to the greater specialization of the modern world) it is now intolerable. We are forced to assume that what we do not like in our time was never good art, and that what appears to us good was always so. If any ancient "philosophical" poetry retains its value, a value which we fail to find in modern poetry of the same type, we investigate on the assumption that we shall find some difference to which the mere difference of date is irrelevant. But if it be maintained that the older poetry has a "philosophic" element and a "poetic" element which can be isolated, we have two tasks to perform. We must show first in a particular case—our case is Dante—that the philosophy is essential to the structure and that the structure is essential to the poetic beauty of the parts ; and we must show that the philosophy is employed in a different form from that which it takes in admittedly unsuccessful philosophical poems. And if M. Valéry is in error in his complete exorcism of "philosophy," perhaps the basis of the error is his apparently commendatory interpretation of the effort of the modern poet, namely, that the latter endeavours "to produce in us a *state*."

The early philosophical poets, Parmenides and Empedocles, were apparently persons of an impure philosophical inspiration. Neither their predecessors nor their successors expressed themselves in verse ; Parmenides and Empedocles were persons

who mingled with genuine philosophical ability a
good deal of the emotion of the founder of a second-
rate religious system. They were not interested
exclusively in philosophy, or religion, or poetry, but
in something which was a mixture of all three ;
hence their reputation as poets is low and as philosophers should be considerably below Heraclitus,
Zeno, Anaxagoras, or Democritus. The poem of
Lucretius is quite a different matter. For Lucretius
was undoubtedly a poet. He endeavours to expound a philosophical system, but with a different
motive from Parmenides or Empedocles, for this
system is already in existence ; he is really endeav-
ouring to find the concrete poetic equivalent for this
system—to find its complete equivalent in vision.
Only, as he is an innovator in this art, he wavers
between philosophical poetry and philosophy. So
we find passages such as :

But the velocity of thunderbolts is great and their
stroke powerful, and they run through their course with
a rapid descent, because the force when aroused first
in all cases collects itself in the clouds and . . . Let us
now sing what causes the motion of the stars. . . .
Of all these different smells then which strike the
nostrils one may reach to a much greater distance than
another. . . .[1]

But Lucretius' true tendency is to express an
ordered vision of the life of man, with great vigour
of real poetic image and often acute observation.

[1] Munro's translation, *passim.*

quod petiere, premunt arte faciuntque dolorem
corporis et dentes inlidunt saepe labellis
osculaque adfligunt, quia non est pura voluptas
et stimuli subsunt qui instigant laedere id ipsum
quodcumque est, rabies unde illaec germina surgunt . . .

                                    medio de fonte leoprum
surgit amari aliquid quod in ipsis floribus angat . . .

nec procumbere humi prostratum et pandere palmas
ante deum delubra nec aras sanguine multo
spargere quadrupedum nec votis nectere vota,
sed mage pacata posse omnia mente tueri.

The philosophy which Lucretius tackled was not
rich enough in variety of feeling, applied itself to
life too uniformly, to supply the material for a
wholly successful poem. It was incapable of complete expansion into pure vision. But I must ask
M. Valéry whether the " aim " of Lucretius' poem
was " to fix or create a notion " or to fashion " an
instrument of power."

Without doubt, the effort of the philsopher proper, the man who is trying to deal with ideas in
themselves, and the effort of the poet, who may be
trying to *realize* ideas, cannot be carried on at the
same time. But this is not to deny that poetry can
be in some sense philosophic. The poet can deal
with philosophic ideas, not as matter for argument,
but as matter for inspection. The original form of a
philosophy cannot be poetic. But poetry can be
penetrated by a philosophic idea, it can deal with
this idea when it has reached the point of immediate

acceptance, when it has become almost a physical modification. If we divorced poetry and philosophy altogether, we should bring a serious impeachment, not only against Dante, but against most of Dante's contemporaries.

Dante had the benefit of a mythology and a theology which had undergone a more complete absorption into life than those of Lucretius. It is curious that not only Dante's detractors, like the Petrarch of Landor's *Pentameron* (if we may apply so strong a word to so amiable a character), but some of his admirers, insist on the separation of Dante's " poetry " and Dante's " teaching." Sometimes the philosophy is confused with the allegory. The philosophy is an ingredient, it is a part of Dante's world just as it is a part of life ; the allegory is the scaffold on which the poem is built. An American writer of a little primer of Dante, Mr. Henry Dwight Sidgwick, who desires to improve our understanding of Dante as a " spiritual leader," says :

To Dante this literal Hell was a secondary matter ; so it is to us. He and we are concerned with the allegory. That allegory is simple. Hell is the absence of God. . . . If the reader begins with the consciousness that he is reading about sin, spiritually understood, he never loses the thread, he is never at a loss, never slips back into the literal signification.

Without stopping to question Mr. Sidgwick on the difference between literal and spiritual sin, we may

affirm that his remarks are misleading. Undoubtedly the allegory is to be taken seriously, and
certainly the *Comedy* is in some way a " moral
education." The question is to find a formula
for the correspondence between the former and the
latter, to decide whether the moral value corresponds
directly to the allegory. We can easily ascertain
what importance Dante assigned to allegorical
method. In the *Convivio* we are seriously informed
that

the principal design [of the odes] is to lead men to
knowledge and virtue, as will be seen in the progress of
the truth of them ;

and we are also given the familiar four interpretations
of an ode : literal, allegorical, moral, and anagogical.
And so distinguished a scholar as M. Hauvette
repeats again and again the phrase " didactique
d'intention." We accept the allegory. Accepted,
there are two usual ways of dealing with it. One
may, with Mr. Sidgwick, dwell upon its significance
for the seeker of " spiritual light," or one may, with
Landor, deplore the spiritual mechanics and find
the poet only in passages where he frees himself
from his divine purposes. With neither of these
points of view can we concur. Mr. Sidgwick magni-
fies the " preacher and prophet," and presents Dante
as a superior Isaiah or Carlyle ; Landor reserves the
poet, reprehends the scheme, and denounces the
politics. Some of Landor's errors are more palpable
than Mr. Sidgwick's. He errs, in the first place,

in judging Dante by the standards of classical epic. Whatever the *Comedy* is, an epic it is not. M. Hauvette well says :

Rechercher dans quelle mesure le poème se rapproche du genre classique de l'épopée, et dans quelle mesure il s'en écarte, est un exércice de rhétorique entièrement inutile, puisque Dante, à n'en pas douter, n'a jamais eu l'intention de composer une action épique dans les règles.

But we must define the framework of Dante's poem from the result as well as from the intention. The poem has not only a framework, but a form ; and even if the framework be allegorical, the form may be something else. The examination of any episode in the *Comedy* ought to show that not merely the allegorical interpretation or the didactic intention, but the emotional significance itself, cannot be isolated from the rest of the poem. Landor appears, for instance, to have misunderstood such a passage as the Paolo and Francesca, by failing to perceive its relations :

In the midst of her punishment, Francesca, when she comes to the tenderest part of her story, tells it with complacency and delight.

This is surely a false simplification. To have lost all recollected delight would have been, for Francesca, either loss of humanity or relief from damnation. The ecstasy, with the present thrill at the remembrance of it, is a part of the torture. Francesca is neither stupefied nor reformed ; she is merely damned ; and it is a part of damnation to experience desires that we can no longer gratify. For in Dante's Hell souls are not deadened, as they mostly are in life ; they are actually in the greatest torment of which each is capable.

E il modo ancor m'offende.

It is curious that Mr. Sidgwick, whose approbation is at the opposite pole from Landor's, should have fallen into a similar error. He says :

In meeting [Ulysses], as in meeting Pier della Vigna and Brunetto Latini, the preacher and the prophet are lost in the poet.

Here, again, is a false simplification. These passages have no digressive beauty. The case of Brunetto is parallel to that of Francesca. The emotion of the passage resides in Brunetto's excellence in damnation —so admirable a soul, and so perverse.

e parve de costoro
Quegli che vince e non colui che perde.

And I think that if Mr. Sidgwick had pondered the strange words of Ulysses,

com' altrui piacque,

he would not have said that the preacher and pro-phet are lost in the poet. " Preacher " and " pro-phet " are odious terms ; but what Mr. Sidgwick designates by them is something which is certainly not " lost in the poet," but is part of the poet.

A variety of passages might illustrate the assertion
that no emotion is contemplated by Dante purely in
and for itself. The emotion of the person, or the
emotion with which our attitude appropriately in-
vests the person, is never lost or diminished, is always
preserved entire, but is modified by the position
assigned to the person in the eternal scheme, is
coloured by the atmosphere of that person's resi-
dence in one of the three worlds. About none of
Dante's character is there that ambiguity which
affects Milton's Lucifer. The damned preserve any
degree of beauty or grandeur that ever rightly per-
tained to them, and this intensifies and also justifies
their damnation. As Jason

> Guarda quel grande che viene !
> E per dolor non par lagrima spanda,
> Quanto aspetto reale ancor ritiene !

The crime of Bertrand becomes more lurid ; the
vindictive Adamo acquires greater ferocity, and the
errors of Arnaut are corrected—

> Poi s'ascose nel foco che gli affina.

If the artistic emotion presented by any episode of
the *Comedy* is dependent upon the whole, we may
proceed to inquire what the whole scheme is. The
usefulness of allegory and astronomy is obvious. A
mechanical framework, in a poem of so vast an am-
bit, was a necessity. As the centre of gravity of
emotions is more remote from a single human action,
or a system of purely human actions, than in drama

or epic, so the framework has to be more artificial and apparently more mechanical. It is not essential that the allegory or the almost unintelligible astronomy should be understood—only that its presence should be justified. The emotional structure within this scaffold is what must be understood—the structure made possible by the scaffold. This structure is an ordered scale of human emotions. Not, necessarily, *all* human emotions ; and in any case all the emotions are limited, and also extended in significance by their place in the scheme.

But Dante's is the most comprehensive, and the most *ordered* presentation of emotions that has ever been made. Dante's method of dealing with any emotion may be contrasted, not so appositely with that of other " epic " poets as with that of Shakespeare. Shakespeare takes a character apparently controlled by a simple emotion, and analyses the character and the emotion itself. The emotion is split up into constituents—and perhaps destroyed in the process. The mind of Shakespeare was one of the most *critical* that has ever existed. Dante, on the other hand, does not analyse the emotion so much as he exhibits its relation to other emotions. You cannot, that is, understand the *Inferno* without the *Purgatorio* and the *Paradiso*. " Dante," says Landor's Petrarch, " is the great master of the disgusting." That is true, though Sophocles at least once approaches him. But a disgust like Dante's is no hypertrophy of a single reaction : it is completed and explained only by the last canto of the *Paradiso*.

> La forma universal di questo nodo,
>   credo ch'io vidi, perchè più di largo
>   dicendo questo, mi sento ch'io godo.

The contemplation of the horrid or sordid or disgusting, by an artist, is the necessary and negative aspect of the impulse toward the pursuit of beauty. But not all succeed as did Dante in expressing the complete scale from negative to positive. The negative is the more importunate.

The structure of emotions, for which the allegory is the necessary scaffold, is complete from the most sensuous to the most intellectual and the most spiritual. Dante gives a concrete presentation of the most elusive :

> Pareva a me che nube ne coprisse
>   lucida, spessa, solida e polita,
>   quasi adamante che lo sol ferisse.
>
> Per entro sè l'eterna margarita
>   ne recepette, com' acqua recepe
>   raggio di luce, permanendo unita.

or

> Nel suo aspetto tal dentro mi fei,
>   qual si fe' Glauco nel gustar dell' erba,
>   che il fe' consorto in mar degli altri dei.[1]

Again, in the *Purgatorio*, for instance in Canto XVI and Canto XVIII, occur passages of pure exposition of philosophy, the philosophy of Aristotle strained through the schools.

> Lo natural e sempre senza errore,
>   ma l' altro puote errar per malo obbietto,
>   o per poco o per troppo di vigore . . .

---

[1] See E. Pound, *The Spirit of Romance*, p. 145.

We are not here studying the philosophy, we *see* it, as part of the ordered world. The aim of the poet is to state a vision, and no vision of life can be complete which does not include the articulate formulation of life which human minds make.

Onde convenne legge per fren porre . . .

It is one of the greatest merits of Dante's poem that the vision is so nearly complete ; it is evidence of this greatness that the significance of any single passage, of any of the passages that are selected as " poetry," is incomplete unless we ourselves apprehend the whole.

And Dante helps us to provide a criticism of M. Valéry's " modern poet " who attempts " to produce in us a *state*." A state, in itself, is nothing whatever.

M. Valéry's account is quite in harmony with pragmatic doctrine, and with the tendencies of such a work as William James's *Varieties of Religious Experience*. The mystical experience is supposed to be valuable because it is a pleasant state of unique intensity. But the true mystic is not satisfied merely by feeling, he must pretend at least that he *sees*, and the absorption into the divine is only the necessary, if paradoxical, limit of this contemplation. The poet does not aim to excite—that is not even a test of his success—but to set something down ; the state of the reader is merely that reader's particular mode of perceiving what the poet has caught in words. Dante, more than any other poet, has succeeded in dealing with his philosophy, not as a theory (in the modern and not the Greek sense of that word) or as his own comment or reflection, but in terms of something *perceived*. When most of our modern poets confine themselves to what they had perceived, they produce for us, usually, only odds and ends of still life and stage properties ; but that does not imply so much that the method of Dante is obsolete, as that our vision is perhaps comparatively restricted.

NOTE.—My friend the Abbé Laban has reproached me for attributing to Landor, in this essay, sentiments which are merely the expression of his dramatic figure Petrarch, and which imply rather Landor's reproof of the limitations of the historical Petrarch's view of Dante, than the view of Landor himself. The reader should therefore observe this correction of my use of Landor's honoured name.